THE PHOTOCOPIABLE RESOURCE Series

Herbert Puchta • Günter Gerngross
Christian Holzmann • Matthew Devitt

Grammar Songs & Raps

For young learners and early teens

Acknowledgements

We would like to thank a number of people without whose support and energy this book would not have happened.
The contribution of Julian Littman cannot be underestimated, for both his compositional brilliance and technical wizardry –
a giant among men!
Special thanks go to all the dulcet-toned young people who sang in the recordings, especially Milly Upton – and the
wonderful Mel Upton and her young people's performance group, Shine, deserve a special mention.

Finally, as always, we are indebted to our editorial and production team for their professionalism and dedication: Caroline
Petherick, Oonagh Wade, Maria Cleary, Christina Freudenschuss, Elisabeth Schipflinger, Francesca Gironi, Elisa Pasqualini,
Amanda Hockin, Barbara Prentiss and Gianluca Armeni.

Herbert Puchta, Günter Gerngross, Christian Holzmann and Matthew Devitt

Grammar Songs and Raps
by Herbert Puchta, Günter Gerngross, Christian Holzmann and Matthew Devitt

© HELBLING LANGUAGES 2012
www.helblinglanguages.com

All rights reserved; no part of this publication may be reproduced, stored in a retrieval system, or transmitted
in any form or by any means, electronic, mechanical, photocopying, recording, or otherwise, without the prior
written permission of the Publishers.
Photocopying of materials from this book for classroom use is permitted.

The publishers would like to thank these sources for their kind permission to reproduce the
following copyright material:
Shutterstock for picture on p72

Edited by Oonagh Wade and Caroline Petherick
Copy edited by Caroline Petherick
Designed by Amanda Hockin, BGP Studio, Pixarte
Cover design by Capolinea
Illustrations by Matteo Buffagni, Svjetlan Junaković, Stefano Fabbri, Giovanni Giorgi Pierfranceschi,
Lorenzo Sabbatini, Doriano Strologo
Printed by Athesia

Every effort has been made to trace the owners of any copyright material in this book.
If notified, the publisher will be pleased to rectify any errors or omissions.

Contents

Introduction		4
1	There's a monster in the forest *(a rap)*	9
2	*To be* party *(a rap)*	14
3	Are you happy? *(a rap)*	19
4	Find the gnomes, Sherlock Groans	23
5	Tea rap	28
6	Pizza rap	32
7	The hungry monster rap	36
8	Generous Joe song	40
9	Peggy Sue	44
10	Midnight on Blueberry Hill	49
11	Robbery at Hanbury Hall	54
12	The story's on TV	59
13	The lion song	64
14	The *going to* song	68
15	The Western star	72
16	The Gang of Four	77
17	The badbad beasts	82
18	All my *have-tos (a rap)*	88
19	*I'm not going to*	93
20	The *some* and *any* rap	97
21	The pyramids	102
22	We are the ghosts	107
23	Please come back	112
24	I'm feeling sick	117
25	It's only a game	121
26	Whatever you can do *(a rap)*	125
27	*Have you ever...?*	130
28	The weatherman *(a rap)*	134
Quick Reference Guide		138
CD contents list		140

Introduction

Grammar Songs and Raps gives you 28 original songs and raps for the ELT classroom with a special focus on supporting the teaching of grammar; they are presented on two audio CDs together with teaching notes and two photocopiable handouts per song. The songs and raps cover a range of structures for beginners and elementary students (A1 and A2 according to the Common European Framework of References). *Grammar Songs and Raps* can be used as support material with any course book or language programme.

How to select a song

The table of contents and the Quick Reference Guide (pp. 138–139) make it easy to select a song or rap according to the language you are planning to teach or practise. Each of the songs or raps has a clear overview with a brief description of the language focus, the language level, a rough estimate of the time you will need to do the activities suggested, and the kind of preparation needed (for example which worksheets you need to copy). This is followed by extensive teaching notes ('In class') with suggestions on how to use each song or rap over two lessons ('Lesson 1' and 'Lesson 2'), each lasting between 10 and 45 minutes ('Time'). The teaching notes are arranged in clear and easy-to-follow steps, with drawings and examples of classroom discourse where necessary, as well as suggestions for extension activities. Answers to all activities and worksheets are included. The lyrics of each song or rap follow the teaching notes.

Photocopiable worksheets

There are up to three worksheets for each song or rap (Worksheets A, B and C).
Worksheet A usually focuses on language and comprehension, with tasks to help students notice, remember and retrieve target structures. Worksheets B and C usually go beyond the song lyrics, with interactive activities and games that encourage students to use the target structures in different contexts. All explanations on classroom management and teaching techniques required in implementing the worksheet activities can be found in the teaching notes.

We are very much aware that the suggestions we are making in this book may need to be adapted for use in your specific classes. You may want to use the activities we are suggesting here, or you may want to develop your own activities around the songs and raps. The activities have been developed in such a way that they can easily be adapted to various language levels.

Introduction

Songs and raps and the teaching and learning of grammar

Young learners and early teens need a good balance of fun and language practice in order to be able to gradually develop language accuracy. Many – or even most – of them do not yet have a deep understanding of grammar rules. That is why many colleagues look for fun ways of supporting their teaching and practising of grammar. At the same time, teachers notice that young learners and teens often show a remarkable ability to pick up and remember chunks of language they come across in stories, pop songs and other forms of texts that they like. Such chunks of language often contain important language structures. Therefore using songs to help students remember strings of words, sentence fragments and sentences can be very valuable practice.

Parents frequently comment that it is amazing how well their kids remember the lyrics of pop songs and regret that when it comes to 'serious learning' memory retrieval seems to happen far less easily. This is not surprising. It's a well-known fact that rhythm, rhyme and catchy tunes have a strong mnemonic function, and make language memorable – a phenomenon that is very successfully employed by people who design TV commercials and radio adverts. The songs and raps in this book have been written in such a way that they contain both useful language (in the form of lexical chunks), and the mnemonic devices mentioned above (rhythm, rhyme and catchy tunes). This means that the chances are high that important language will be remembered well by the students, and more easily transferred to their long-term memory.

Motivation

Many colleagues have noticed that authentic pop songs are not always greeted with enthusiasm by their students. On the face of it this sounds strange, but on further investigation it turns out that the teachers' choices are rarely identical with the choices students themselves would make, whereas teachers are often not happy about songs that students would like to hear in the foreign language classroom. This is because the songs are either too demanding in terms of the language level, or their content and language turn out to be problematic from a pedagogical point of view; as a colleague recently commented, it seems quite difficult to find any authentic song lyrics these days without references to sex and drugs, or which don't contain swearing!

All lyrics have been specifically written for the foreign language class. They can be used with beginners and elementary students. We have tried to get as much humour and fun into the lyrics as possible, as humour and fun are important support systems facilitating motivation and long-term memory recall.

Introduction

Luckily, when we work with young learners and early teens we can count on their enthusiasm for songs if their quality is good. Young learners and early teens are also normally keen to sing along with a song or join in a rap if the tune is catchy and/or the rhythm is riveting. The songs and raps you will find in this material have been developed with a specialist and trialled carefully in young learners' and early teens' classrooms. We are happy to say that the feedback we got from students was very positive, and colleagues working with our trial classes reported that their students became very engaged in singing along with the songs.

Language learning and songs

When students listen to a song or rap for the first time, they naturally want to understand what the lyrics are all about. If the song or rap is engaging, they will want to sing or chant along. Thus, songs are about developing the students' listening comprehension and about repeating important words, structures and chunks of language. The process of understanding the lyrics of a song is an interesting one as it often involves the gradual interpretation of the language in the song. When students listen for the first time they may not understand a lot. But if the song is intriguing, they will make their hypotheses about the meaning of the lyrics, and when they listen a second or a third time they can verify their hypothesis or change their initial interpretations. Thus, their comprehension gradually grows and they learn an important skill – to be persistent with trying to understand meaning and not to give up when they cannot understand everything immediately.

Songs and raps are also ideal for developing pronunciation, word stress and intonation patterns. In a song, important lexis, structures and chunks of language get repeated time and time again without the process becoming boring for the students. Imitation is an important element in that process – the more fun and engaging the students find a song or rap to be the more they will develop positive feelings about the language in the song or rap. This kind of affective dimension plays a very important role in the process of the students' learning of a foreign language.

The flashcards on the CD-ROM

Flashcards are useful in teaching the meaning of new words and in getting students to memorise them better. Flashcards are great timesavers and mean teachers do not have to draw on the board or look for or make suitable pictures. This is why CD 2 that comes with this book is not only an Audio CD, but a hybrid CD-ROM that offers you (on top of the songs it contains) the PDFs of all the flashcards we recommend using in the teaching notes.
We recommend you download the flashcards onto the hard drive of your computer and print the ones you need for whatever song you have selected for your class. Alternatively, you can print the flashcards directly from CD 2 without downloading the files.

Introduction

Teaching the songs

It is easier to hum or sing along with a song than to sing without the support of the audio, especially when the song we want to join in with is in a foreign language. This is why it is advisable to play the songs several times before students are asked to join in and sing along. When students hear a song several times, it will be easier for them to sing. Likewise, we might notice that students find it much easier to sing along with a song when the song gets revised in a follow-up lesson than they did the first time they came across it.

How to use the karaoke version of the raps

On the Audio CDs, you will find 18 songs and 10 raps. For each of the raps there is also a karaoke version on the Audio CD; this is a version without voices, where students hear just the musical instruments.

When you want to use the karaoke version of a rap, make sure your students have listened to the version with the voice(s) often enough to find it easy to chant along with the music. Many of the raps are in the form of a dialogue between a singer/speaker and a chorus of children, so when you use the karaoke version you may want to agree beforehand with the students in your class who says what. If you use the Pizza rap on p. 33, to give just one example, you could get half the class to do the first verse, the other half the second verse, and the whole class to do the chorus:

Half the class:
She doesn't eat carrots,
She doesn't eat rice,
She doesn't like onions:
"Peas aren't nice!"

Other half:
She doesn't eat burgers –
"No, they aren't good!"
She doesn't eat chicken –
"Just my favourite food –

Whole class:
"And that's pizza with cheese
Pizza with cheese
Pizza with cheese
Can I have one, please?
Pizza with cheese
Pizza with cheese
Can I have one, please?"

Introduction

Then get the students to carry on in a similar way.

Likewise, when a rap is in the form of a dialogue, one group (e.g. all the girls in the class) could ask the questions, whereas another group (e.g. all the boys) give the answers. An example of this would be the first part of the Hungry Monster rap on p. 37.

Girls: An egg?
Boys: No thanks.
Girls: A sausage?
Boys: No thanks.
Girls: An orange?
Boys: No thanks.
Girls: A yoghurt?
Boys: No thanks.
Girls: An apple?
Boys: No thanks.
Girls: A mango?
Boys: No thanks.
Girls: Aren't you hungry?
Boys: Yes, of course.
But I eat desks, and doors, and wooden floors.

Later, you could also encourage your students to change the words slightly, thus helping them develop their creative thinking skills.

Songs and raps help to relax and overcome shyness

When students can sing or chant along with a song or a rap, they can more easily enjoy the psychological shelter they get from their peer group being involved in a harmonious and unifying activity. This way, shyer students will easily overcome their inhibitions and enjoy imitating the sounds of the foreign language, and the rhythm of a song or rap can have a very stimulating and engaging effect on the group dynamics of a classroom. Thus, singing a song or doing a rap together is fun and can at the same time have a very positive effect on interaction among the students on the one hand and the students with their teacher on the other. This is because students will find it easier to relate well to their classmates and to their teacher if they enjoy their lessons.

We have enjoyed writing the songs and the activities and materials around them. It is our hope that you and your students enjoy using them as much as we did creating them!

there is/there are

1 There's a monster in the forest
a rap

Track 01/02

Language focus	*there is/there are*
Level	Post-beginners / A1
Time	Lesson 1: 30 minutes
	Lesson 2: about 20 minutes
Materials	CD1 – Track 01: audio recording of the rap
	CD1 – Track 02: karaoke version of the rap
	CD2/CD-ROM part: *There's a monster in the forest* Flashcards
	Lesson 1: a copy of the lyrics for each student; a copy of Worksheet A per student
	Lesson 2: a copy of Worksheet B per two students, several pairs of scissors

In class

Lesson 1

1. Teach or revise the following words using the flashcards provided:

   snake, frog, rabbit, dog, fox, hamster, owl, bear.

2. Play the game Guess My Animal; write the following language prompts on the board:

   A: *Is it a snake?*   B: *Yes, it is./No, it isn't.*

   Think of one of the animals and tell your students they should try to guess it. The student who has guessed the animal comes to the front of the classroom and thinks of another animal that the classmates have to guess.

3. Give each student a copy of Worksheet A. Tell them to listen to the rap and write the words from the box in the gaps, and tell them you will play the rap twice. Then, when you play it the second time, stop it frequently so that the students have ample time to copy the words from the box and write them into the gaps.

4. Tell your students that you are going to give them information about one of the animals on their worksheet. They should guess which of the animals you are talking about. Say, e.g., *It's long. It has no feet. I'm scared of it. What is it?*

5. Ask your students to form two groups, A and B. Hand out a copy of the lyrics. Ask them to read the lyrics aloud in their groups. Then play the rap, and the students join in.

Answers   snakes, frogs, rabbits, dogs, foxes, hamsters, owls, bear, owls

there is/there are

Extension

1. When the students are already familiar with several forms of asking questions, they can play a more elaborate form of Guess My Animal.

   A: Can it fly/run fast/climb trees?   B: Yes, it can./No, it can't.
   A: Has the animal got four legs? wings? a tail? fur?   B: No, it hasn't./Yes, it has.
   A: Does the animal eat …?   B: No, it doesn't./Yes, it does.
   A: Does the animal live in the water? in Africa?

2. You can encourage students to take over your role from step 4. Individual students describe an animal. The others try to guess it.

   A: My animal has got four legs. It's green or grey. It lives in the water.
   B: Is it a frog?
   A: No, it isn't.
   B: Is it a crocodile?
   A: Yes, it is.

Lesson 2

1. Introduce or revise the following additional animal words:

   cat, cow, horse, mouse, sheep.

   Teach the plural of the words, emphasizing the plural of *mouse* and *sheep*. Then play the following guessing game with your students. Show them a number with your fingers by holding up e.g. three fingers. Then mime a mouse. Elicit from the students the sentence: *There are three mice.* Show them the number one, and mime a cat. Elicit from the students the sentence: *There's a cat.* Ask students to take your part.

2. Ask your students to work in pairs. Hand out one copy of Worksheet B to each pair. Ask them to cut it into two parts so that each student has one part. Write the following language on the board:

   In my picture there are three … In my picture there's only one … .

3. Ask students in pairs to compare pictures A and B. Tell your students that they are not allowed to look at their partner's worksheet.

Extensions

The students describe their worksheet from memory. Write the following on the board: *In my picture there are …, there's …*

Use the karaoke version as suggested on pp. 7-8.

There's a monster in the forest

(Help!
What's the matter?
Look! There's a monster!)

A There's a monster in this forest.
   There's a monster with six eyes.
   Help me, help me, there's a monster!
   We must run! Come on, you guys!

B Ha! There's no monster!
   Ha! There's no monster!
   There are snakes, there are frogs,
   There are rabbits, there are dogs,
   There are foxes, hamsters, owls,
   And there's a bear – it's over there!
   Yeah!
   But there's no monster in the forest.

A There is a monster in the forest!

(Now listen, and say what's in the forest.
One, two, three.)

A Monster – there's a monster.
B Monster – there's a monster.
A There's a monster with six eyes.
B There's a monster with six eyes.

A Rabbits – there are rabbits.
B Rabbits – there are rabbits.
A Foxes – there are foxes.
B Foxes – there are foxes.
A Frog – there's a frog.
B Frog – there's a frog.
A Dog – there's a dog.
B Dog – there's a dog.

(And there are three owls – look, you guys,
that's our monster with six eyes!
Oh! How stupid!!)

there is/there are

There's a monster in the forest | Worksheet A

Complete the gaps.

| owls   bear   rabbits   frogs   foxes   owls   hamsters   dogs   snakes |

Help!
What's the matter?
Look! There's a monster!

A There's a monster in this forest.
   There's a monster with six eyes.
   Help me, help me, there's a monster!
   We must run! Come on you guys!

B Ha! There's no monster!
   Ha! There's no monster!
   There are _____,
   there are _____,
   There are _____,
   there are _____,
   There are _____,
   _____, _____,
   And there's a _____
   – it's over there!
   Yeah!
   But there's no monster in the forest.

A There is a monster in the forest!

Now listen, and say what's in the forest.

A Monster – there's a monster.
B Monster – there's a monster.
A There's a monster with six eyes.
B There's a monster with six eyes.

A Rabbits – there are rabbits.
B Rabbits – there are rabbits.
A Foxes – there are foxes.
B Foxes – there are foxes.
A Frog – there's a frog.
B Frog – there's a frog.
A Dog – there's a dog.
B Dog – there's a dog.

   And there are three _____
   – look, you guys,
   that's our monster with six eyes!
   "Oh! How stupid!!"

There's a monster in the forest | Worksheet B

Find the differences between the two pictures.

forms of *to be*

2 *To be* party
a rap

Track 03/04

Language focus Forms of *to be*

Level Beginners / A1

Time Lesson 1: about 30 minutes
Lesson 2: about 25 minutes

Materials CD1 – Track 03: audio recording of the rap
CD1 – Track 04: karaoke version of the rap
CD2/CD-ROM part: *To be party* Flashcards
Lesson 1: a copy of the lyrics for each student; a copy of Worksheet A per student. For step 4, make an enlarged copy of the lyrics, number the lines for your own reference, and then cut the lines into individual strips. For step 7, cut out six paper stars (sheriffs' stars) and have a fastener or a piece of sellotape for each one.
Lesson 2: a copy of Worksheet B per group of three students.

In class

Lesson 1

1. Teach or revise the following words using the flashcards provided: *clown, sheriff, princess, cowboy*.

Write the words on the board.

2. Tell the students that you are going to play a rap to them. Tell them to listen carefully and try to remember as much as possible. Ask them to say the words, phrases or sentences they remember. Write these on the board.

3. Hand out a copy of the lyrics. Ask the students to listen and read along.

4. Show each lyric line strip very briefly and elicit the line from the students. Then play the rap again, and the students join in.

5. Ask the class to form a big circle. Inside the circle on the left arrange two chairs next to one another, and two chairs that stand alone. Ask a boy and a girl to sit on the two chairs and a boy and a girl on the individual chairs.

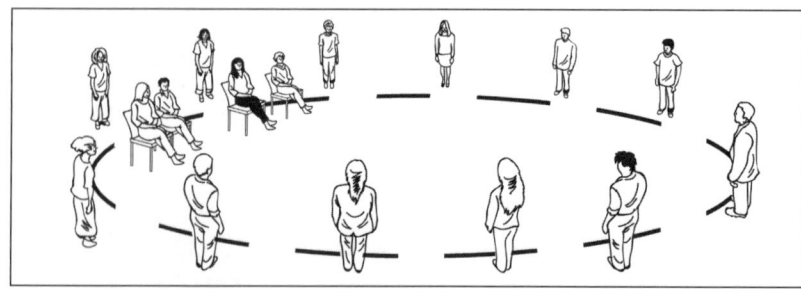

14   Puchta/Gerngross/Holzmann/Devitt | Grammar Songs & Raps | © Helbling Languages

6. Arrange two chairs on the right of the circle. Sit down on one, and ask a student to sit down on the other.

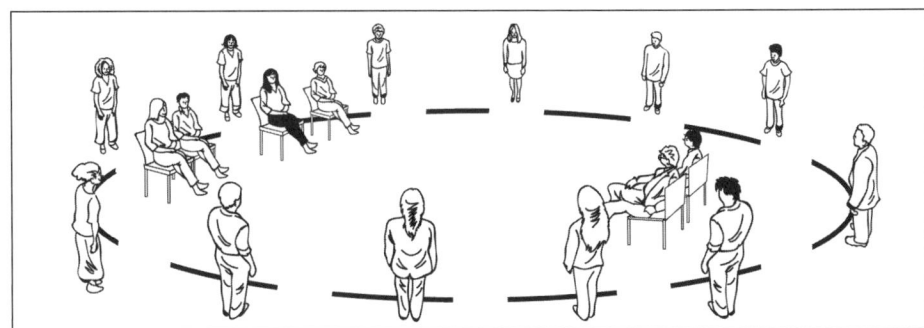

7. Now hand the paper stars to all the students sitting on the chairs. Fasten one on your own clothes, and fasten the others to the students' clothes. Then point at yourself and say: *I'm a sheriff*. Ask the student sitting next to you to say with you: *We're sheriffs*. Point at the two students and say: *They're sheriffs*. Then point to the girl and say: *She's a sheriff* and to the boy, and say: *He's a sheriff*. Now just do the pointing several times and ask the class to say the sentences.

8. Then hand each student a copy of Worksheet A. Tell them to look at the pictures and the sentences, then number the sentences to match the pictures. Say a number and ask individual students to read out the respective sentence.

Answer
2 We're cowboys.   6 They're cowboys.   4 He's a clown.
3 She's a princess.   1 I'm a sheriff.   5 They're clowns.

Lesson 2

1. Introduce the words *pilot* and *doctor*, using the flashcards provided.

2. Ask the students to work in groups of three. Two students, A and B, play the game, and the third student, C, is the referee. Hand a copy of Worksheet B to each group. Student A starts and points at a picture; B says the sentence, e.g. *I'm a princess*. If B's sentence is correct, the referee gives B a point. Then B points at a picture and A says the sentence. They play ten rounds and then the referee announces the winner or says if it was a draw.

3. Now C joins the game and A becomes the referee. Finally A and C play, and B becomes the referee.

Extensions

Discuss with your class whether they would like to perform the rap in front of an audience, e.g. their parents. If they are keen on doing that, rehearse the rap including mime and dance steps.

Use the karaoke version as suggested on pp. 7-8.

forms of to be

To be party

I'm the sheriff,
You're the clown,
He's a cowboy,
Please sit down.
Clap, clap, now you rap!

I'm the sheriff,
You're the clown,
He's a cowboy,
Please sit down.
Clap, clap, now you rap!

She's a princess,
It's great fun,
Clap your hands
Everyone.
Clap, clap, now you rap!

She's a princess,
It's great fun,
Clap your hands
Everyone.
Clap, clap, now you rap!

We're so happy,
You're so cool.
There's a party
At our school.
Clap, clap, now you rap!

We're so happy,
You're so cool.
There's a party
At our school.
Clap, clap, now you rap!

Lots of girls,
Lots of boys.
They're so loud –
What a noise!
Clap, clap, now you rap!

Lots of girls,
Lots of boys.
They're so loud –
What a noise!

(Sssssshhhh!
Quiet, everyone:
And now really fast – here we go!)
(repeat rap)

(Woooooo!
And now even faster!)
(repeat rap)

To be party | Worksheet A

forms of to be

Match, and write numbers.

| We're cowboys. | They're cowboys. | He's a clown. |
| She's a princess. | I'm a sheriff. | They're clowns. |

forms of *to be*

To be party | Worksheet B

Say the sentence.

forms of to be

3 Are you happy?
a rap

Track 05/06

Language focus Forms of *to be:* negative and questions, vocabulary: feelings

Level Post-beginners / A1

Time Lesson 1: 20 minutes
Lesson 2: about 30 minutes

Materials CD1 – Track 05: audio recording of the rap
CD1 – Track 06: karaoke version of the rap
CD2/CD-ROM part: *Are you happy?* Flashcards
Lesson 1: a copy of Worksheet A per student
Lesson 2: a copy of Worksheet B per student

In class

Lesson 1: Are you happy?

1. Introduce or revise the following words using the flashcards provided or mime: *hot, cold, happy, sad, bored, angry, scared, hungry.*

2. Ask a student to come to the front. Whisper one of the words in their ear. The student mimes the words and the classmates try to guess the word.

3. Play the rap to the students. Hand out Worksheet A. Tell them to circle the correct words.

4. Play the rap again and ask the students to check. Then play the rap a third time and ask the students to join in.

Lesson 2: A guessing game

1. Stand in front of the class and show Worksheet B to your students. Tell them that you're going to choose one picture. Put the worksheet face down, and ask them to guess which person you're thinking of and write on the board:

Is it a girl?/boy? Are there two people?

forms of to be

When they have guessed correctly, ask the student to guess how the person/the people in the picture feels/feel. Write on the board:

Is he/she sad? Are they angry?

2. Hand out the worksheets. Ask the students to play the game in pairs. Student A places an eraser, a coin or any other small object on one of the pictures; B cannot see A's worksheet. A says: *Guess*. B tries to find out whether the object is on a boy, a girl or two people. Then B tries to guess how the person or the people in the picture feels/feel. A keeps a record of the number of guesses.

3. Now the students change roles. The one who needs fewer guesses is the winner of one round. Tell your students to play five rounds.

Extension

Use the karaoke version as suggested on pp. 7-8.

Are you happy?

Ice cream, ice cream,
Give the kids some ice cream –
They're hot!

Yehhhhhhh
Mmmmmmmm
Oooooohhhhh

Are you happy?
No, I'm not.
Are you cold?
No, I'm hot.

Is she happy?
No, she's not.
Is she cold?
No, she's hot.

Is he happy?
No, he's not.
Is he cold?
No, he's hot.

Are you happy?
No, we're not.
Are you cold?
No, we're hot.

Are they happy?
No, they're not.
Are they cold?
No, they're hot.

Ice cream, ice cream,
Give the kids some ice cream –
They're hot!

(Let's ask the question again.)

Are you happy?
...
(repeat to end)

Puchta/Gerngross/Holzmann/Devitt | Grammar Songs & Raps | © Helbling Languages

Are you happy? | Worksheet A

Listen and circle the correct words.

Are you **happy / sad**?
No, I'm not.
Are you **hot / cold**?
No, I'm **hot / cold**.

Is she **sad / happy**?
No, she's not.
Is she **hot / cold**?
No, she's **cold / hot**.

Is he **scared / happy**?
No, he's not.
Is he **angry / cold**?
No, he's **sad / hot**.

Are you **hungry / happy**?
No, we're not.
Are you **bored / cold**?
No, we're **hot / sad**.

Are they **scared / happy**?
No, they're not.
Are they **cold / bored**?
No, they're **hot / angry**.

Ice cream, ice cream, give the kids some ice cream! They're **hot**!

forms of *to be*

A guessing game | Worksheet B

Guess which person I'm thinking of. Guess how they feel.

Present simple

4 Find the gnomes, Sherlock Groans

Track 07

Language focus Present simple
Level Post-beginners / A1
Time Lesson 1: 45 minutes
Lesson 2: about 25 minutes
Materials CD1 – Track 07: audio recording of the song
CD2/CD-ROM part: *Find the gnomes, Sherlock Groans* Flashcard
Lesson 1: a copy of the lyrics for each student; a copy of Worksheet A per student
Lesson 2: a copy of Worksheet B per student, some red pens

In class

Lesson 1

1. Ask the students if they know the name of a famous detective. If no student comes up with the name *Sherlock Holmes*, tell them that he was a very **clever** detective. Then say that the name of the detective in the song they are going to hear is Sherlock Groans. Tell them the meaning of the verb *groan* in their mother tongue. Explain that Sherlock Groans is a very **clumsy** detective.

2. In the song, they are going to hear that Lady Grey wants Sherlock Holmes to find her garden gnomes. Explain *garden gnome* using the flashcard provided.

3. Then introduce or revise the following verbs or phrases using gestures and mime:

   phone a person
   leave the house
   look for something
   hit your head
   bump into a tree
   climb a tree
   fall out of a tree
   shout

4. Say one of the phrases, and ask the students to mime it. Then tell them to work in pairs: A says a phrase and B tries to mime it, then they swap roles.

5. Play the song to the students. Hand out Worksheet A. Tell them to put the pictures in the correct order by numbering them. Play the song again and ask them to check.

Puchta/Gerngross/Holzmann/Devitt | Grammar Songs & Raps | © Helbling Languages   23

Present simple

6. Draw a grid with nine squares on the board. The grid is a graphic representation of the worksheet. Ask the students to tell you the number for each square.

7. Hand out the lyrics, then play the song again getting the students to sing along.

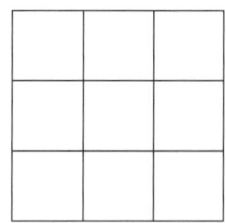

Answer

4	8	3
7	5	1
9	2	6

Lesson 2

1. Introduce or revise the following phrases: *have breakfast, get out of bed, wash your face, drop something*. Use pictures and/or mime the phrases. Write the phrases on the board.

2. Hand out Worksheet B. Tell the students to think for a minute of a new story, using the pictures. They can start anywhere.

3. Ask a student to try to tell a story, using the pictures as a stimulus. If necessary reformulate without correcting in order to provide the correct language.

   Student: Sherlock Groans leave house.
   Teacher: OK, Sherlock Groans leaves his house. And then?
   Student: He go in park.
   Teacher: Right, he goes to the park.
   Student: Sherlock Groans find a …. (student can't remember the word)
   Teacher: He finds a gnome.
   Student: Then he drop … he drops the gnome. Oh no!
   Teacher: Great story! Thanks, (name of student).

4. Ask the students to work in pairs. Ask them to number the pictures of their story in red.

5. The students then tell their story to their partners. Remind them again to begin like this: *First … Then he … And then … Finally…* . Their partners listen and number the pictures of their partner's story on their own worksheet in another colour. Then they swap.

6. Finally they compare their worksheets. Ask individual students to tell their story.

Extension

The students write their stories. The teacher corrects them and they rewrite them. Then they stick them on a wall of the classroom. Each student tries to read as many stories as possible and they give positive feedback, e.g.:

I like your story. It's great!
Good idea.
Nice.
Love it!

Present simple

Find the gnomes, Sherlock Groans

*(How many kinds of gnomes can I see
in my English country garden?
None! They've all been stolen!
Bring me the telephone!)*

Lady Grey
Phones Sherlock Groans.
She wants to know
About her gnomes.
And Sherlock Groans,
The clever man,
Tells Lady Grey
He's got a plan.

*Find the gnomes,
Sherlock Groans.
Find the gnomes,
Sherlock Groans.*
(repeat)

He leaves his house,
Goes to the park.
He looks for gnomes,
But it's too dark.
He hits his head,
Is he okay?
"Oh goodness me!"
Says Lady Grey.

Chorus

He looks for cats,
But he finds rats,
Bumps into trees,
"Oh, stop it, please!"
He climbs a tree
And he falls out
And then he hears
The lady shout:

Chorus

Lady Grey
Tells Sherlock Groans
She wants to know
About her gnomes.
And Sherlock Groans
Tells Lady Grey
That it's not a lucky day.

(Where are my gnomes?)

Present simple

Find the gnomes, Sherlock Groans | Worksheet A

Put the pictures in the correct order. Write the numbers in the boxes.

Find the gnomes, Sherlock Groans | Worksheet B

Present simple

Tell your story.

3rd person singular

5 Tea rap

Track 08/09

Language focus	3rd person singular *s*, present simple
Level	Post-beginners / A1
Time	Lesson 1: 15 minutes
	Lesson 2: 15 minutes
Materials	CD1 – Track 08: audio recording of the rap
	CD1 – Track 09: karaoke version of the rap
	CD2/CD-ROM part: *Tea rap* Flashcard
	Lesson 1: a copy of Worksheet A per student
	Lesson 2: a copy of Worksheet B per student

In class

Lesson 1

1. Show the students a picture of an eccentric-looking man using the flashcard provided.

2. Ask the students some questions about the man (see examples below) and write the students' answers around the picture.

   - *What's his name?*
   - *How old is he?*
   - *What's his favourite colour?*
   - *What's his favourite food?*
   - *What's his favourite drink?*

3. Hand out a copy of Worksheet A. If necessary, explain the meaning of the words *breakfast*, *lunch* and *dinner*. Play the rap and ask the students to complete the gaps. Then elicit the correct answers from the students by asking questions.

Answer What's the man's name? Philip, Earl of Grey
What does he eat for breakfast? He eats three eggs and some bread.
What does he eat for lunch? He eats cabbage, peas and rice.
What does he eat for dinner? He eats fish and potatoes.
What's his favourite drink? He loves tea.

Lesson 2

1. Play the rap again. Ask the students to listen and then to call out words they remember from the lyrics, e.g. *Earl of Grey, three eggs and some bread for breakfast*, etc.

3rd person singular

2. Hand out Worksheet B. Ask students to fill the gaps with the verbs from the box at the top. You may not want to give them any help at this point – just let them fill in the verbs. Quite a few of your students will probably copy the verbs in their infinitive form.

3. Play the rap again and ask students to check.

4. Elicit the correct forms of the verbs by getting students to read out their answers. When they have finished, write the following on the board and get students to complete it:
For breakfast, I eat bread and butter
Philip, Earl of Grey …

5. Ask students why, when we talk about habits, it is 'I **eat**' and 'Philip, Earl of Grey **eats**'; then elicit a rule from them, e.g. *When we talk about another person we say he/she eat**s**/drink**s**/like**s*** … (Note that this discussion might have to be done in the students' mother tongue.)

6. Tell them to complete the stem sentences in the lower part of Worksheet B and read their sentences out in class.

Extension

Use the karaoke version as suggested on pp. 7-8.

Tea rap

(Listen, children, this is the tea rap.)

Philip, Earl of Grey,
Drinks tea, night and day.
What does Philip eat for breakfast,
Tell me, what?

He eats three eggs
And he eats some bread,
He drinks some tea
And goes back to bed.

Tea at seven,
Tea at nine,
Tea at one
Is really fine.

Tea at three
And five and eight,
Tea at midnight –
Tea is great!

(I love my tea!)

Philip, Earl of Grey,
Drinks tea, night and day.
What does Philip eat for lunch,
Tell me, what?

He eats some cabbage
With some peas and rice.
He drinks some tea –
Tea is always nice!

Chorus

(He's a greedy man.
Aye.)

Philip, Earl of Grey,
Drinks tea, night and day.
What does Philip eat for dinner,
Tell me, what?

He drinks some tea,
He eats some fish,
He eats potatoes and
Then makes a wish:

Chorus

(Delicious!)

3rd person singular

Tea rap | Worksheet A

Listen and complete.

Menu

This is Ph _____, E _____ of G _____ .

Breakfast Three _____

some b _____

Lunch some c _____

some p _____

some r _____

Dinner some f _____

some p _____

E _____ of G _____ ♡ _____ .

Tea rap | Worksheet B

3rd person singular

1 Complete. Use the correct form of the verb. Then listen and check.

| drink | go | eat | eat | eat | Drink | |
| Drink | drink | Drink | eat | drink | make | eat |

Tea rap

Philip, Earl of Grey,
_____ tea, night and day.
What does Philip eat for breakfast,
Tell me, what?

He _____ three eggs
And he _____ some bread,
He _____ some tea
And _____ back to bed.

Tea at seven,
Tea at nine,
Tea at one
Is really fine.

Tea at three
And five and eight,
Tea at midnight –
Tea is great!

Philip, Earl of Grey,
_____ tea, night and day.
What does Philip eat for lunch,
Tell me, what?

He _____ some cabbage
With some peas and rice.
He _____ some tea –
Tea is always nice!

Chorus

Philip, Earl of Grey,
_____ tea, night and day.
What does Philip eat for dinner,
Tell me, what?

He _____ some tea
He _____ some fish
He _____ potatoes and
Then _____ a wish:

Chorus

2 Write sentences about yourself and the Earl of Grey. Use *eat, drink* and *love*.

eat / drink:
For breakfast, I _____
_____
Philip, Earl of Grey, _____
_____
For lunch, I _____
_____
Philip, Earl of Grey, _____
_____
For dinner, I _____
_____
Philip, Earl of Grey, _____
_____

love:
I _____
_____
Philip, Earl of Grey, _____
_____

Puchta/Gerngross/Holzmann/Devitt | Grammar Songs & Raps | © Helbling Languages **PHOTOCOPIABLE**

Negation 3rd person

6 Pizza rap

Track 10/11

Language focus Negation, 3rd person singular present simple

Level Post-beginners / A1

Time Lesson 1: 30 minutes
Lesson 2: about 30 minutes

Materials CD1 – Track 10: audio recording of the rap
CD1 – Track 11: karaoke version of the rap
CD2/CD-ROM part: *Pizza rap* Flashcards
Lesson 1: a copy of Worksheet A per student
Lesson 2: a copy of Worksheet B per pair

In class

Lesson 1

1. Introduce or revise the following words using the flashcards provided:
   carrots, rice, onions, burger, pizza, cheese, chicken, peppers, broccoli, fish, spinach, peas and *beans*.

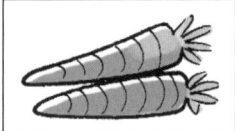    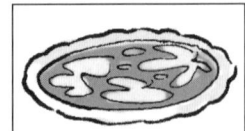
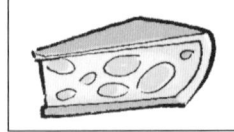 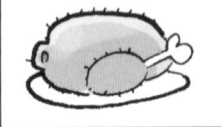 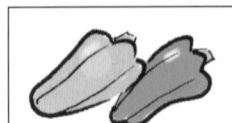  
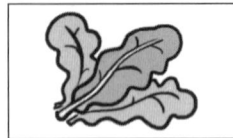  

2. Play the following game. Tell the students that you are thinking of one of the words in step 1. Ask them to guess it. Write the following language on the board:

   Is it the peppers? Yes, it is./No, it isn't.
   Is it red/green/etc?
   Is it a vegetable?

   When they have guessed three words, ask the students to work in pairs.

   As an alternative you could write the first letter of a word on the board. The students try to guess it.

3. Hand out Worksheet A. Play the rap to the students. Tell them to tick the correct picture. Play the rap again and ask them to check.

4. Play the rap again and ask the students to join in.

Negation 3rd person

Answer carrots, rice, onions, peas, burgers, chicken, peppers, fish, broccoli, spinach, beans

Lesson 2

1. Hand out Worksheet B. Tell your students to finish the face on the left and to give it a name.

2. Tell your students that they should decide what the person eats and what they don't eat. They decide by ticking either the happy or the sad face under each food.

3. Write *Her/His name is … She/He doesn't eat … She/He eats ….* on the board. Ask your students to work in pairs. First A says the name of their person and says what he/she eats/doesn't eat, while B writes the name under the face on the right and ticks either the happy or sad face for each food choice. Then B talks about his/her person, and A writes the name below the face and ticks the sad or happy face for each food item.

4. Finally, they compare their pictures, and A and B finish the faces on the right-hand side.

Extensions

The students write down what their person eats/doesn't eat.

Use the karaoke version as suggested on pp. 7-8.

Pizza rap

(Hello everyone! This is my friend,
Hungry Helen – say hello, Helen.
"Hello!"
She's got a problem.)

She doesn't eat carrots,
She doesn't eat rice,
She doesn't like onions:
"Peas aren't nice!"

She doesn't eat burgers –
"No, they aren't good!"
She doesn't eat chicken –
"Just my favourite food –

"And that's pizza with cheese
Pizza with cheese
Pizza with cheese
Can I have one, please?
Pizza with cheese
Pizza with cheese
Pizza with cheese
Can I have one, please?"

(Oh Helen, you're such a fussy eater!)

She doesn't like peppers,
She doesn't like fish,
She doesn't like broccoli:
"That's not what I wish."

She doesn't like spinach –
"No, that isn't good."
She doesn't like beans –
"Just my favourite food –

Chorus

Puchta/Gerngross/Holzmann/Devitt | Grammar Songs & Raps | © Helbling Languages

Pizza rap | Worksheet A

Tick ✓ the correct picture.

Hungry Helen

She doesn't eat  / ,

She doesn't eat  / ,

She doesn't like  / :

"  /  aren't nice!"

She doesn't eat 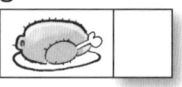 / 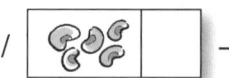 –
"No, they aren't good!"

She doesn't eat / –
"Just my favourite food –

And that's pizza with cheese
Pizza with cheese
Pizza with cheese
Can I have one, please?
Pizza with cheese
Pizza with cheese
Pizza with cheese
Can I have one, please?"

She doesn't like 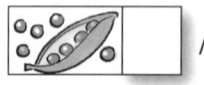 / 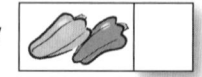 ,

She doesn't like  / 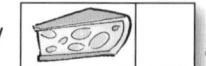 ,

She doesn't like  / 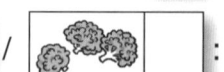 :
"That's not what I wish."

She doesn't like 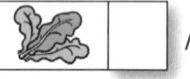 /  –
"No, that isn't good."

She doesn't like 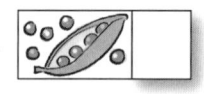 / 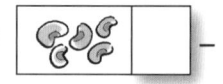 –
"Just my favourite food –

And that's pizza with cheese
Pizza with cheese
Pizza with cheese
Can I have one, please?
Pizza with cheese
Pizza with cheese
Pizza with cheese
Can I have one, please?"

Pizza rap | Worksheet B

Negation 3rd person

Draw the face and fill in the boxes with what the person eats or doesn't eat. Then tell your partner.

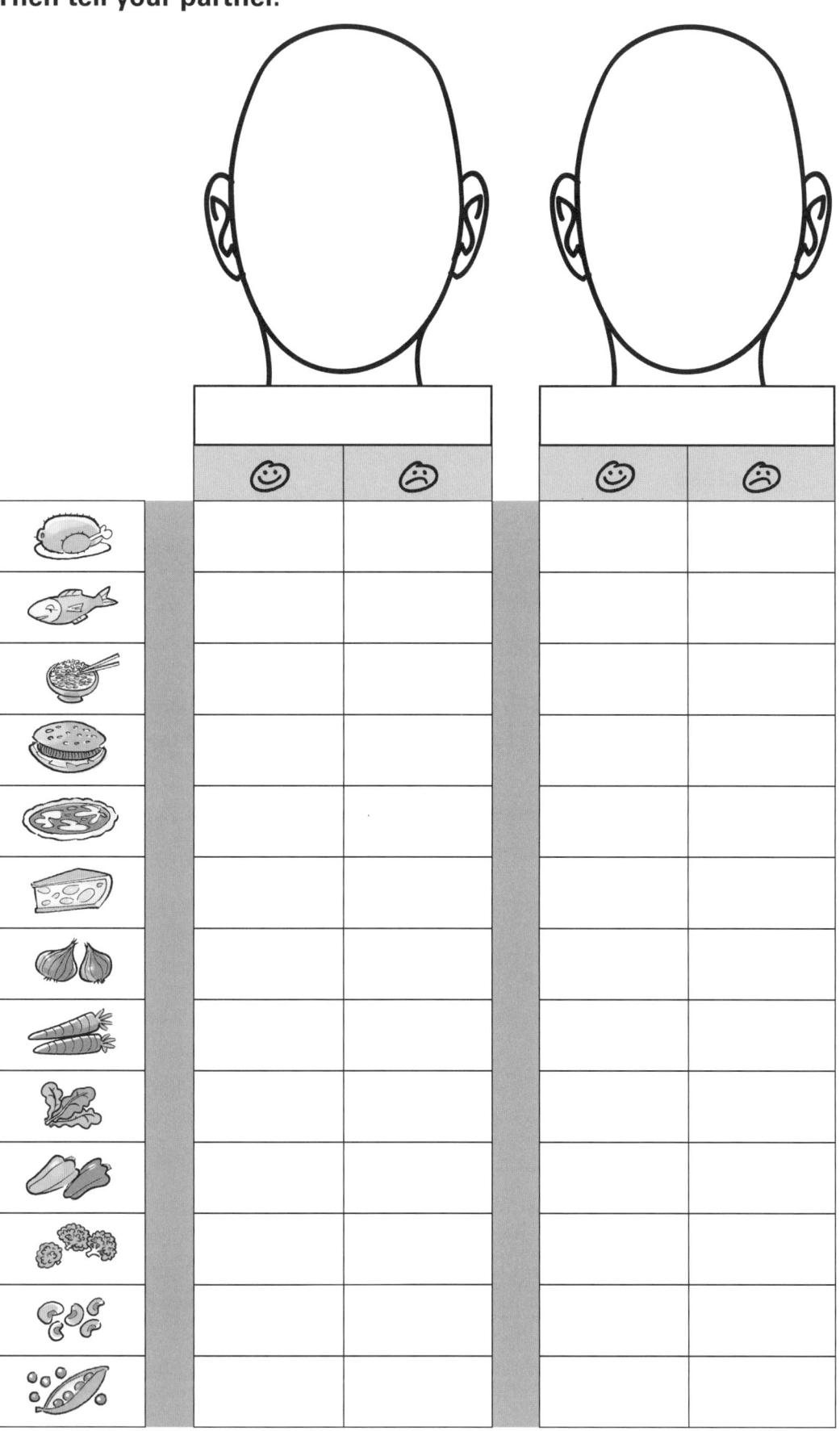

a/an

 The hungry monster rap

Track 12/13

Language focus *a/an*

Level Beginners / A1

Time Lesson 1: 20 minutes
Lesson 2: about 10 minutes

Materials CD1 – Track 12: audio recording of the rap
CD1 – Track 13: karaoke version of the rap
CD2/CD-ROM part: *The hungry monster rap* Flashcards
Lesson 1: a copy of the lyrics for each student; a copy of Worksheet A per student
Lesson 2: a copy of Worksheet B per student; cut each sheet in half. Each student will need to bring in 16 tokens (coins, buttons etc.)

In class

Lesson 1

1. Introduce or revise the following words using the flashcards provided: *egg, sausage, orange, yoghurt, apple, mango.*

2. Play the rap to the students. Hand out the lyrics of the rap. Ask the students to read it aloud. Then play the rap again and ask the students to join in. First the girls ask the questions, and the boys play the part of the monster. Then the girls play the monster and the boys ask the questions. Then tell the students to put away the text.

3. Hand out Worksheet A. Tell them to complete the words.

4. Play the rap again and ask the students to check.

Answer egg, sausage, orange, yoghurt, apple, mango

Lesson 2

1. Hand out Worksheet B, 1. Tell your students to find the six words and to circle them in red.

2. When they have finished, tell your students to circle the indefinite articles *a* and *an* in another colour. They should then draw lines from *a/an* to the food words.

3. Ask individual students to read out what they have connected.

4. Hand out Worksheet B, 2. Tell your students to play a game in pairs. Student A should not be able to see B's worksheet, and vice versa. A puts a token on a picture and says the word. Now this word is blocked for player B, which means that he/she must not say it. Then it is B's turn. B puts a token on a picture and says the word. Now that picture is blocked for player A. Then it is A's turn again etc. The game ends when, e.g., A says a word that has been blocked by B; then B is the winner.

a/an

Extension

Use the karaoke version as suggested on pp. 7-8.

Answer

A	N	F	P	O	Y	F
B	M	Z	N	R	O	W
S	A	U	S	A	G	E
R	N	Z	Y	N	H	G
F	G	S	N	U	U	G
Q	O	M	L	E	R	K
A	P	P	L	E	T	A

a: mango, sausage, yoghurt
an: orange, egg, apple

The hungry monster rap

(Listen, girls and boys
What's that noise?
It's coming from over there.
Ahhhh!
Look – a monster!
"Whhahahahaah! I'm hungry!"
Just a minute ...)

An egg?
No thanks.
A sausage?
No thanks.
An orange?
No thanks.
A yoghurt?
No thanks.
An apple?
No thanks.
A mango?
No thanks.
Aren't you hungry?
Yes, of course!
But I eat desks, and doors, and wooden floors.

(repeat whole rap x 2)

(He's eaten my desk and my doll!
Do you want ketchup with that?
Oooh, I've got a tummyache!)

Puchta/Gerngross/Holzmann/Devitt | Grammar Songs & Raps | © Helbling Languages

a/an
The hungry monster rap | Worksheet A

Complete the words.

Listen, girls and boys
What's that noise?
It's coming from over there.
Ahhhh – Look, a monster!
"Whhahahahaah! I'm hungry!"
Just a minute …

An e_____?
No thanks.

A s_____?
No thanks.

An o_____?
No thanks.

A y_____?
No thanks.

An a_____?
No thanks.

A m_____?
No thanks.

Aren't you hungry?
Yes, of course!
But I eat desks, and doors, and wooden floors.

Listen, girls and boys
What's that noise?
It's coming from over there!
Ahhhh – Look, a monster!
"Whhahahahaah! I'm hungry!"

a/an

The hungry monster rap | Worksheet B

1 **Find the words and draw lines.**

A	N	F	P	O	Y	F
B	M	Z	N	R	O	W
S	A	U	S	A	G	E
R	N	Z	Y	N	H	G
F	G	S	N	G	U	G
Q	O	M	L	E	R	K
A	P	P	L	E	T	A

2 **Play the game.**

Puchta/Gerngross/Holzmann/Devitt | Grammar Songs & Raps | © Helbling Languages PHOTOCOPIABLE

Object pronouns

8 Generous Joe song

CD1 Track 14

Language focus Object pronouns

Level Post-beginners / A1

Time Lesson 1: 20 minutes
Lesson 2: about 30 minutes

Materials CD1 – Track 14: audio recording of the song
CD2/CD-ROM part: *Generous Joe song* Flashcards
Lesson 1: a copy of the lyrics for each student; a copy of Worksheet A per student
Lesson 2: a copy of Worksheet B per student

In class

Lesson 1

1. Play the song to the students.

2. Hand out Worksheet A. Tell the students to find out what Generous Joe gives away. Tell your students to circle the pictures showing the things Joe gives away.

3. Play the song again and ask the students to check if they have circled the correct pictures.

4. Hand out the lyrics, then play the song again getting the students to sing along. Then play the song again. Ask the students to join in.

Answer bike, jam, pen, shoe

Lesson 2

1. Introduce or revise the following words using the flashcards provided:

   CD, book, pen, paintbox, pencil case, guitar, car, cap, hat, T-shirt, sweater, jeans.

   Ask a student to come to the front. Whisper one of the words in their ear. The student mimes the words, and the classmates try to guess the word.

2. Hand out Worksheet B. Tell the students to imagine that they give each of the people a present. Tell your students to decide what to give to the people. Then they draw lines from the people to the presents.

3. Now the students work in pairs. A asks B, e.g., *What about Jane?* B: *I gave her a pen.* If your students haven't learnt the past tense, explain the meaning of *gave* in their mother tongue. *What about Frank and Tim? I gave them a ...* Write the two dialogues on the board. Then B starts asking A.

4. Ask individual students to say what presents they gave to the people.

Object pronouns

Generous Joe song

Joe, Joe, Joe's so generous,
He gives all his things away.
Hey, can't you see, oh no!
There's nothing left for Joe!

There is good old Mike:
Joe gives him a bike.
There is lovely Pam:
Joe gives her some jam.

Chorus

There are Frank and Sue and Ken:
Joe gives them his pen.
And then I say, "Hey you!"
So Joe gives me his shoe.

Chorus (x 2)

Object pronouns

Generous Joe song | Worksheet A

Find out what Joe gives away. Circle the pictures.

42   **PHOTOCOPIABLE** Puchta/Gerngross/Holzmann/Devitt | Grammar Songs & Raps | © Helbling Languages

Giving presents | Worksheet B

Who gets which present? Draw lines.

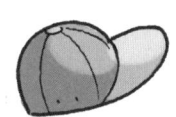

Question words

9 Peggy Sue

CD1 Track 15

Language focus	Question words
Level	Post-beginners / A1
Time	Lesson 1: 30 minutes
	Lesson 2: about 30 minutes
Materials	CD1 – Track 15: audio recording of the song
	CD2/CD-ROM part: *Peggy Sue* Flashcards
	Lesson 1: a copy of the lyrics for each student; a copy of Worksheet A per student
	Lesson 2: a copy of Worksheet B per student

In class

Lesson 1

1. Teach or revise the following words with the help of the flashcards provided or translation: *pet, zoo, potatoes, boa constrictor, meat, week*.
   Show the words with the help of the flashcards. The students say the words.

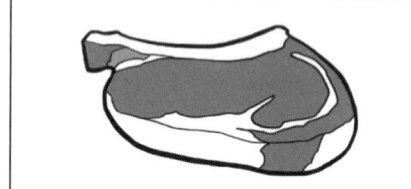

2. Write the first letter of each word on the board and ask the students to say the words.

3. Give each student a copy of Worksheet A. Tell them to listen to the song and tick the sentences True or False. Play the song as often as necessary for them to tick.

4. Then play it one more time, stopping it frequently so that the students have enough time to check.

5. Hand out a copy of the lyrics. Ask them to read the lyrics aloud. Then play the song again, and the students join in.

6. Then ask the students to look at exercise 2. Revise or introduce the names of the 12 animals. Tell your students to draw six of the twelve animals in Peggy Sue's new zoo. When they have finished drawing their animals, they work in pairs and try to find out what their partner has put into Peggy Sue's new zoo. Give them an

example:

A: *Has Peggy Sue got a ...?*

B: *Yes, she has./No, she hasn't.*

Answers
1. F Her name is Sally Sue.
2. T She works in a zoo.
3. F She has got three pets.
4. T Her pet is a snake.
5. F The snake eats potatoes and rice.
6. F The snake loves meat.
7. T Her friend meets Peggy Sue once a week.
8. T Peggy Sue and her friend ride on the snake.
9. F The other kids want to ride too.
10. T Peggy Sue is very cool.

Lesson 2

1. To sensitize your students to question words, ask them to make a simple grid.

What	
Who	
How often	
When	

2. Play the song once again, asking them to count the number of times they hear the question words by making a mark in the respective row whenever they hear one.

3. Hand out Worksheet B. Tell the students to work in pairs; A asks the questions, B answers and A takes notes. Then they swap roles.

4. When they've completed the questionnaire, ask your students to get into groups of four. Each student works with a new partner, telling them about their previous partner; so A tells C about B, while B tells D about A. Then C tells A about D, and D tells B about C.

5. The students complete the sentences with the information their new partners are telling them.

6. Ask individual students to talk about their partners.

Extension

The students think of more questions with *What, Who, How often, When, Where*. Write the new questions on the board. Then ask the students to form a circle. Two volunteers sit in the middle of the circle and A asks B the new questions.

Question words

Peggy Sue

Who's that girl?
Peggy Sue.
What does she do?
She works in a zoo.

(Sing along
It won't take long)

That's Peggy, Peggy, Peggy Sue
She's so cool, so cool, that's true!
Peggy, Peggy, Peggy Sue
She's so cool, so cool, that's true!

What's her pet?
A boa constrictor.
What's its name?
Emanuel Victor.

(Sing along
It won't take long)

Chorus

That snake she's got,
What does it eat?
Potatoes and beans –
It doesn't eat meat.

(Sing along
It won't take long)

Chorus

How often do you
Meet Peggy Sue?
Just once a week
At the zoo.

And when you meet,
What do you do?
You and your friend
Peggy Sue?

We climb on the snake
To have a ride
And all the other kids
Run and hide.

Help!!!

Chorus

So cool, so cool, that's true!
She's so cool, so cool, that's true!
That's Peggy Sue!

Peggy Sue | Worksheet A

Question words

1 Tick ✓ True or False.

		True	False
1	Her name is Sally Sue.		
2	She works in a zoo.		
3	She has got three pets.		
4	Her pet is a snake.		
5	The snake eats potatoes and rice.		
6	The snake loves meat.		
7	Her friend meets Peggy Sue once a week.		
8	Peggy Sue and her friend ride on the snake.		
9	The other kids want to ride too.		
10	Peggy Sue is very cool.		

2 Draw and ask.

Question words

Peggy Sue | Worksheet B

1 Questionnaire: ask your partner and take notes.

1	Who is your favourite singer, sportsperson or actor?	
2	What is your favourite food?	
3	What do you usually have for breakfast?	
4	Where do you keep your favourite toys?	
5	When do you usually get up in the morning?	
6	Where do you meet your friends?	
7	When do you go to bed?	
8	How often do you go to the cinema?	
9	What is your favourite sport?	
10	How often do you do sports a week?	

2 Write about your partner.

Her/His favourite singer/actor is_____

Her/His favourite food is _____

She/He has _____for breakfast.

She/He keeps her/his favourite toys _____

She/He gets up at _____

She/He meets her/his friends _____

She/He goes to bed at _____

She/He goes to the cinema _____

Her/His favourite sport is _____

She/He does _____sports a week.

Present continuous

10 Midnight on Blueberry Hill

CD1 Track 16

Language focus	Present continuous
Level	Post-beginners / A1
Time	Lesson 1: 20 minutes
	Lesson 2: about 30 minutes
Materials	CD1 – Track 16: audio recording of the song
	CD2/CD-ROM part: *Midnight on Blueberry Hill* Flashcards
	Lesson 1: a copy of Worksheet A per student
	Lesson 2: a copy of Worksheet B per two students

In class

Lesson 1

1. Teach or revise the following words using the flashcards provided:
   castle, rat, spider, ghost, moon, fox, owl.

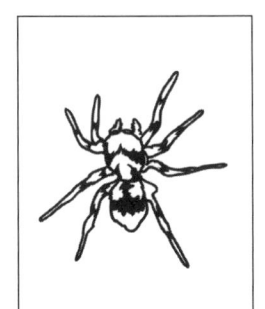

2. Show the words with the help of the flashcards. The students say the words.

3. Put the flashcards one after the other in a pile, and while you're doing this say: *Number one is castle, number two is rat, number three is spider*, etc.

   Then ask your students: *What was number one?* etc. The students try to remember the words.

4. Play the song and ask the students to listen carefully. Then hand out a copy of Worksheet A to each student. Ask them to unscramble the letters and write the words in the gaps.

Puchta/Gerngross/Holzmann/Devitt | Grammar Songs & Raps | © Helbling Languages

Present continuous

5. Then play the song again and stop it frequently so that the students have enough time to check what they have written.

6. Ask them to read the lyrics aloud. Then play the song and the students sing along.

Answers midnight, castle, time, friends, rats, moon, wonderful, drums, carrot, monsters, dancing, fun, sing

Lesson 2

1. Teach or revise the following phrases with the help of mime and gestures, and write them on the board:

ride a bike	*play ping pong*	*close the door*
play computer games	*eat spaghetti*	*open a window*
watch TV	*get out of bed*	*read*
play the drums	*put on a sweater*	*write*
dance	*take off a cap*	*drink something*
sing a song		

2. Ask one of your students to mime one of the phrases; ask, e.g.: *Are you getting out of bed?* Elicit: *Yes, I am./No, I'm not.*

3. Write on the board: *Are you playing the drums? Yes, I am./No, I'm not.*

4. Cover the phrases on the board. Ask your students to get into groups of four. One student mimes an action he or she remembers from the list, and the others guess what she/he is doing.

5. Tell your students to work in pairs. Hand out Worksheet B to each pair. Write the following dialogue on the board:

   A: *I think Owen is dancing.*
   B: *I think so too./I don't think so. I think he is playing ping pong.*
   A: *Max and Abby are reading books.*
   B: *I think so too./I don't think so. I think they are writing.*

6. Ask individual students about the silhouettes e.g.:

   You: *(Name of student), what about number 1?*
   Student: *I think Mike is eating something.*

Answers
1. Mike is eating spaghetti.
2. Eva is playing the drums.
3. Rebecca and Judith are riding their bikes.
4. Naomi is singing a song.
5. Kelly and Charles are watching TV.
6. Lara is getting out of bed.
7. Oscar is putting on a sweater.
8. Max and Abby are playing computer games.
9. Emily is closing the door.
10. Daniel is taking off his cap.
11. Owen is dancing.
12. Tyler and Ryan are playing ping pong.
13. Connor is reading.
14. John and Anna are writing.
15. Christopher is drinking something.
16. Denise is opening the window.

Extension

The students write down what they think the children are doing.

Present continuous

Midnight on Blueberry Hill

(ooh, aah)

*It's midnight on Blueberry Hill
And the castle is coming to life.
It's midnight on Blueberry Hill
And we're having the time of our life.*

Archie the ghost is riding his bike
With his friends Camilla and Lee.
The spiders are playing computer games
And the rats are watching TV.

Chorus

(Oh yes we are – ooh, aah)

It's midnight on Blueberry Hill
And the moon is shining so bright.
It's midnight on Blueberry Hill
It's such a wonderful sight.

Arnie the fox is playing the drums,
And the owl is dancing along,
The rabbit is singing the carrot song.
The monkeys are playing ping pong.

Chorus

(haha, there's more to come! ooh, aah)

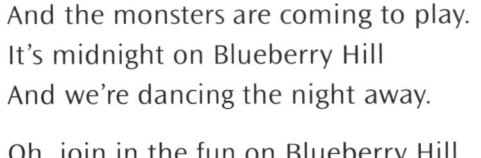

It's midnight on Blueberry Hill
And the monsters are coming to play.
It's midnight on Blueberry Hill
And we're dancing the night away.

Oh, join in the fun on Blueberry Hill,
Where the cats are playing some rock.
Come on, and sing and dance along,
From midnight to one o'clock.

Chorus (x 2)

Present continuous

Midnight on Blueberry Hill | Worksheet A

Listen and write the words.

It's _____ on Blueberry Hill (inmthdig)
And the _____ is coming to life. (slatec)
It's midnight on Blueberry Hill
And we're having the _____ of our life. (emit)

Archie the ghost is riding his bike
With his _____ Camilla and Lee. (renisdf)
The spiders are playing computer games
And the _____ are watching TV. (tasr)

Chorus

It's midnight on Blueberry Hill
And the _____ is shining so bright. (nomo)
It's midnight on Blueberry Hill
It's such a _____ sight. (fwlodnrue)

Arnie the fox is playing the _____, (smurd)
And the owl is dancing along,
The rabbit is singing the _____ song. (tarocr)
The monkeys are playing ping pong.

Chorus

It's midnight on Blueberry Hill
And the _____ are coming to play. (tsomesrn)
It's midnight on Blueberry Hill
And we're _____ the night away. (cadnign)

Oh, join in the _____ on Blueberry Hill, (nfu)
Where the cats are playing some rock.
Come on, and _____ and dance along, (gnis)
From midnight to one o'clock.

Chorus
(repeat)

Present continuous

Midnight on Blueberry Hill | Worksheet B

Work in pairs. Say what the people are doing.

1. Mike 
2. Eva 
3. Rebecca and Judith 
4. Naomi 
5. Kelly and Charles 
6. Lara 
7. Oscar 
8. Max and Abby 
9. Emily 
10. Daniel 
11. Owen 
12. Tyler and Ryan 
13. Connor 
14. John and Anna 
15. Christopher 
16. Denise

Puchta/Gerngross/Holzmann/Devitt | Grammar Songs & Raps | © Helbling Languages **PHOTOCOPIABLE**

Past tense of *to be*

11 Robbery at Hanbury Hall

CD1 Track 17

Language focus	Past tense of *to be* + questions
Level	Post-beginners / A1 – Elementary / A2
Time	Lesson 1: 20 minutes
	Lesson 2: 20 minutes
Materials	CD1 – Track 17: audio recording of the song
	Lesson 1: a copy of Worksheet A per student
	Lesson 2: copy Worksheet B onto card, and cut out the set of cards

In class

Lesson 1

1. Ask students to tell you where they were yesterday/an hour ago/a week ago, e.g.:

   You: Melike, tell me, where were you yesterday at seven?
   Melike: (I was) at home.

2. Ask students to work in pairs and ask each other where they were yesterday/an hour ago/a week ago.

3. Listen to some of the answers in class. Ask student A about student B, e.g.:

   You: Luigi, where was Sophie last week?
   Luigi: She was at home. She had the flu.

4. Hand out Worksheet A. Tell the students they have to find out from the song what the four people answer to the Inspector's questions.

5. Play the song. Ask the students to listen carefully and write down the answers.

6. One student then points to a different student each time and asks the four questions, e.g.: *Where were you, Mr….?*. The other student answers as if they were one of the four people from the song: *I was …* etc.

7. Ask students to do the second task on the worksheet. Remind them to ask and answer all questions in past tense.

Answers

1. Mr White: I was in the hall.   Mrs Black: I don't know anything.
   Lady Brown's son: I don't know and I don't care.   Lady Brown: Oh, (Inspector,) that's not fair.
2. Where was the cat? It was on the sofa.   Where were the books? They were on the floor.
   Where were the glasses/spectacles? They were on the desk.
   Where were the shoes? They were under a chair. Where was the pipe? It was on a shelf.

Past tense of *to be*

Lesson 2

1. Ask a student where he/she was yesterday. The student answers the question and then asks another student. Continue for 1–2 minutes.

2. Play the song. Then repeat it, with a small group singing the Inspector's questions while the rest of the class sings the chorus.

3. Hand out the cards from Worksheet B. Each student gets a card; if there are fewer than 15 students, some students can have two cards, and if there are more, then some students will need to share.

4. Explain the game: one student starts the game by reading out the question on their card. The others have to listen carefully. Only one card has the correct answer to that question.

5. The student with that card reads out the answer, and then continues by reading out the question on their card. In turn, the student who has got the answer to that question reads it out, and continues by reading out the question they have etc.

Answers

Q: Where was Inspector Clue at half past six? A: At half past six the Inspector was in the hall.
Q: Where were the Browns on Friday? A: The Browns were in London on Friday.
Q: Where were Lady Brown and her aunt during the robbery? A: Lady Brown and her aunt were in the library during the robbery.
Q: Where was Inspector Clue at lunchtime? A: At lunchtime he was in the large hall.
Q: Where was Sir Frederick on his holiday? A: On his holiday he was in Scotland.
Q: Where was Sir Frederick when there was a party next door? A: He was at the party, of course!
Q: Where was Inspector Clue after his visit to Hanbury Hall? A: After his visit to Hanbury Hall he and his sergeant were at the police station.
Q: Where were Lady Brown and her aunt for dinner? A: For dinner, she and her aunt were at the Hanbury Hotel.
Q: Where were the Browns after the weekend? A: After the weekend they were back in their country home.
Q: Where were Lady Brown and her aunt on Sunday morning? A: On Sunday morning they were at the police station.
Q: Where were the robbers in the morning? A: In the morning the robbers were on their way to France.
Q: Where were the robbers yesterday? A: Yesterday they were already in jail.
Q: Where were the robbers at midnight? A: At midnight the robbers were long gone.
Q: Where was Sir Frederick at lunchtime? A: Sir Frederick was asleep in the living room at lunchtime.
Q: Where were the Browns during the night? A: During the night they were fast asleep in their bed.

Extension

Revising words for places and asking questions.

In class, write on the board a list of places (both indoors and outdoors), e.g. *hall, library, kitchen, bedroom, garden, pond, woods*, etc.

Students work in pairs. Student A thinks of an object, e.g. a mobile phone, and 'hides' it in one of the places by writing on a piece of paper where the mobile is, without showing to their partner. A then says: *Oh dear, yesterday I lost my mobile!* B has up to five guesses to work out where it was found, e.g.:

A: *Oh dear, yesterday I lost my mobile! But then I found it again.*
B: *Really? Where was it? Was it in the library?*
A: *No, it wasn't.*
B. *Was it in the garden?*
A: *Yes, it was.*

Past tense of *to be*

Robbery at Hanbury Hall

(I wonder what time it is. I shall go and look at the clock in the library. Wait a minute! It's not there! There's been a robbery!)

Robbery, robbery at Hanbury Hall.
Robbery, robbery! Go and call
Inspector Clue
He's the man for you.
(He's the man for you.)
(repeat)

Mr White, and where were you?
In the hall? And is that true?
Mrs Black, what do you know?
Nothing? Really? Is that so?

Chorus (x 2)

Where were you at nine, my lady?
I don't know – in the kitchen maybe.
Where were you sir? Were you also there?
I don't know and I don't care.

Chorus (x 2)

Lady Brown, once again,
Where were you at nine p.m.?
And your son? Was he there?
Oh, Inspector, that's not fair!

Chorus

Robbery, robbery at Hanbury Hall,
Inspector Clue, he knows it all,
He's so clever, clever Clue.

(I'm the most brilliant mind in Scotland Yard.
I know the answer – what about you?)

Robbery at Hanbury Hall | Worksheet A

Past tense of *to be*

1. Listen to the song. Inspector Clue asks a few questions. Write down what the people answer.

Mr White
Where were you, Mr White?
I _____

Mrs Black
What do you know, Mrs Black?
I _____

Lady Brown's son
Where were you, sir?
I _____

Lady Brown
Where was your son, Lady Brown?
Oh, _____

2. Inspector Clue asks about the missing objects. Write down the questions and the answers he got.

Where was the clock? Oh I see, it was on the wall.

Where _____ ?   Where _____ ?
It _____ the sofa.   They _____ .
Where _____ ?   Where _____ ?
They _____ .   It _____ .
Where _____ ?
They _____ .

Puchta/Gerngross/Holzmann/Devitt | Grammar Songs & Raps | © Helbling Languages **PHOTOCOPIABLE**

Past tense of to be

Robbery at Hanbury Hall | Worksheet B

Cut out the cards.
Play the game.

Have you got the answer to the question?

WHERE?

Q: Where was Inspector Clue at half past six?	**Q:** Where were the Browns on Friday?	**Q:** Where were Lady Brown and her aunt during the robbery?
A: On his holiday he was in Scotland.	**A:** Sir Frederick was asleep in the living room at lunchtime.	**A:** For dinner, she and her aunt were at the Hanbury Hotel.

Q: Where was Inspector Clue at lunchtime?	**Q:** Where was Sir Frederick on his holiday?	**Q:** Where was Sir Frederick when there was a party next door?
A: After his visit to Hanbury Hall he and his sergeant were at the police station.	**A:** During the night they were fast asleep in their bed.	**A:** At midnight the robbers were long gone.

Q: Where was Inspector Clue after his visit to Hanbury Hall?	**Q:** Where were Lady Brown and her aunt for dinner?	**Q:** Where were the Browns after the weekend?
A: Lady Brown and her aunt were in the library during the robbery.	**A:** The Browns were in London on Friday.	**A:** He was at the party, of course!

Q: Where were Lady Brown and her aunt on Sunday morning?	**Q:** Where were the robbers in the morning?	**Q:** Where were the robbers yesterday?
A: In the morning the robbers were on their way to France.	**A:** After the weekend they were back in their country home.	**A:** At lunchtime he was in the large hall.

Q: Where were the robbers at midnight?	**Q:** Where was Sir Frederick at lunchtime?	**Q:** Where were the Browns during the night?
A: Yesterday they were already in jail.	**A:** At half past six the Inspector was in the hall.	**A:** On Sunday morning they were at the police station.

Puchta/Gerngross/Holzmann/Devitt | Grammar Songs & Raps | © Helbling Languages

Past tense

12 The story's on TV

CD1 Track 18

Language focus Past tense

Level Post-beginners / A1 – Elementary / A2

Time Lesson 1: 15 minutes
Lesson 2: 15 minutes

Materials CD1 – Track 18: audio recording of the song
Lesson 1: a copy of Worksheet A per student
Lesson 2: a copy of the lyrics for each student; a copy of Worksheets B and C per student
Extension 1: ask students to bring magazines, scissors and glue sticks, or provide these yourself
Extension 2: mobile phone cameras/video cameras; printer for photos, computer to show videos

In class

Lesson 1

1. Ask students about what they watch on TV. Expect them to give you titles, mostly. Ask them how much of it is real, e.g.: *Are these real/true stories? Can these stories happen in real life?*

2. Tell them you are going to play them a song about some stories from TV that are not true. Ask the students to remember as many words as possible. Play the song. After listening, they call them out. Write the words on the board. Ask the students how many stories of one sentence each they can make out of the words.

3. Ask students to work in pairs. Tell them: *Think of a story (maybe from TV) that is not true. Imagine you are in the story. Tell each other about it. Listen carefully so you can tell the class your partner's story later.*

   For example: *One day I found a beautiful golden ring. I gave it to my friend and she was very happy about it and she kissed me.*

4. In class, ask a few students to share the stories their partners told them. (*One day John found a beautiful golden ring …*)

5. Hand out Worksheet A. Play the song again, and ask students to do the tasks and compare their answers in pairs. Then ask them to write down sentences that go with the pictures. Check the answers in class.

Answer

Puchta/Gerngross/Holzmann/Devitt | Grammar Songs & Raps | © Helbling Languages

Past tense

Lesson 2

1. Hand out the lyrics and play the song. Ask students to sing along: form two groups, one of which sings the chorus.

2. Hand out Worksheet B. The students fill in the words from the box and replace the pictures with words. Ask them to check in pairs.

3. Hand out Worksheet C. Ask students to write their own stories. Tell them to think of their story from the previous lesson and ask them to make it a little bit longer. Tell them that 5–7 lines would be ideal for a story. If students can't think of anything, write the words *Story on TV* on the board and brainstorm ideas with them. Then ask them to pick an idea from the board and write a little story.

4. Ask students to swap their stories. Tell them to read their partner's story. Tell them they can give it one, two or three smileys, depending on how much they liked it.

5. Ask individual students to read out their stories.

Answers

1 a) TV, sunny, rock guitar, star, girl, Nile, night, crocodile, fight, little house, space, underwear
1 b) went, played, lived, tried, won, met

Extension 1

Ask students to get together in groups and make a collage/a cartoon strip of a story they can think of.

Extension 2

Some of these little stories can be filmed. Students work in groups and decide which pictures they want to take/sequences they want to film. Their work can either be displayed on the wall or viewed on the computer. If they have photos, ask them to print them out, then stick them on paper and put speech bubbles with them. If they film a story, they should record some dialogue.

The story's on TV

1 On a sunny day
He just went away.
He played the rock guitar –
He became a star.

*Can't you see, see, see?
The story is not real – the story's on TV.*
(repeat)

2 On a dark dark night
She had a fight
With a crocodile
That was in the Nile.

Chorus (x 2)

3 From my little place
They went into space –
Met some Martians there
In their underwear.

Chorus (x 2)

The story's on TV | Worksheet A

Past tense

1. The song is about three stories. Listen and number the pictures 1, 2 and 3. Use each number more than once.

2. Listen to the song again and write six short sentences about the pictures, e.g.: *The man went away.*

Puchta/Gerngross/Holzmann/Devitt | Grammar Songs & Raps | © Helbling Languages **PHOTOCOPIABLE**

Past tense

The story's on TV | Worksheet B

1 Listen to the song, then

a) write the words under the drawings

b) fill in the correct past forms of the words from the box.

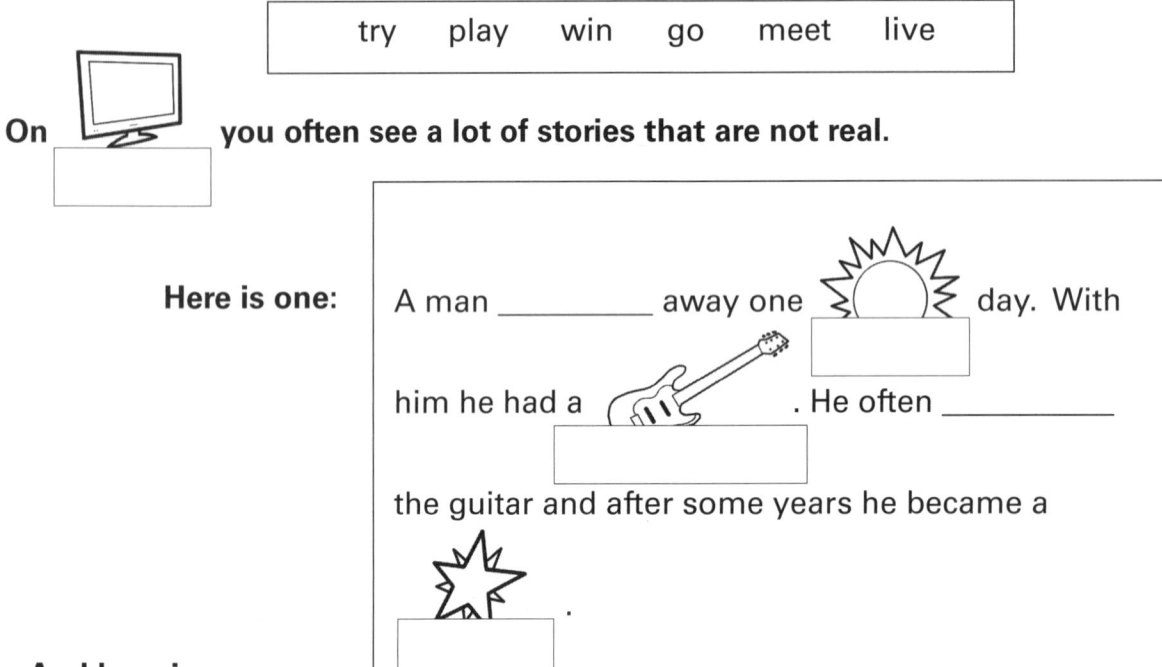

| try play win go meet live |

On [TV] you often see a lot of stories that are not real.

Here is one:

A man _____ away one [sun] day. With him he had a [guitar]. He often _____ the guitar and after some years he became a [star].

And here is another one:

A [girl] _____ near the River [Nile]. One dark [night] she went for a walk near the river when a [crocodile] jumped out and _____ to eat her. But the girl had a [fight] with the crocodile and she _____.

And here is a third one:

A man lived alone in a [house]. One day two friends came to see him. From the man's place they went into [space]. There they _____ some Martians. The Martians were in their [underpants]!

None of these stories are real – they're only on TV.

Past tense

The story's on TV | Worksheet C

Now write your own little story for TV!

Animals

13 The lion song

CD1 Track 19

Language focus	Vocabulary: animals
Level	Post-beginners / A1
Time	Lesson 1: 20 minutes Lesson 2: about 15 minutes
Materials	CD1 – Track 19: audio recording of the song CD2/CD-ROM part: *The lion song* Flashcards Lesson 1: a copy of the lyrics for each student; a copy of Worksheet A per student Lesson 2: a copy of Worksheet B per group of 4–6 students, and one envelope per group. Cut out the rectangles with the pictures and animal names, and put each cut-up worksheet in an envelope.

In class

Lesson 1

1 Teach or revise the following names for animals using the flashcards provided:

   jackal, snake, elephant, antelope, ant, shark, duck, crocodile, hippo, monkey, kangaroo, camel, mouse – mice, gnu, rabbit, frog, buffalo, tiger, polar bear

2. Give each student a copy of Worksheet A. Tell them to write an animal name into each of the squares of bingo card A.

3. Tell the students that you are going to play a song to them. Tell them to listen carefully and cross out all the animal names on their bingo card that they can hear in the song. Tell them to stand up and shout *Bingo!* whenever they have crossed out three animals in a row (diagonally, vertically or horizontally).

4. Repeat the bingo game, this time using bingo card B.

5. Hand out the lyrics, then play the song again getting the students to sing along.

Lesson 2

1. Put the students into groups of 4–6. Give each group one of the envelopes. Ask them to open the envelopes, take out the little cards and put them all face down on their desks. One student starts; they pick up one card and read out or say the word for the animal. If their card shows the animal picture, they need to find the corresponding card showing the word and vice versa. They pick up another card. If that card is the corresponding one, the student can carry on playing. If it isn't, it's the next student's turn.

2. When the game is over, the student who has the most cards is the winner.

The lion song

One, two, three, four,
ROAAAARRR!
This is the lion song,
The song – of the strong.

(Let's hear them hands clapping.)

Well, jackals, snakes and elephants,
Antelopes and small red ants.
Sharks and ducks and crocodiles
Animals for miles and miles –
I'm the king
So let us sing …

Chorus
(Keep them hands clapping.)

Hippos, monkeys, kangaroos,
Camels, mice and big, big gnus.
Rabbits, frogs and buffaloes,
A tiger and a polar bear,
Lots of animals everywhere –
And I'm the king
So let us sing …

Chorus
(Don't you stop clapping, kids.)

Well, jackals, snakes and elephants,
Antelopes and small red ants
Sharks and ducks and crocodiles
Animals for miles and miles –
I'm the king
So let us sing …

Chorus
(Come on, keep clapping, we're almost there.)

Hippos, monkeys, kangaroos,
Camels, mice and big, big gnus.
Rabbits, frogs and buffaloes,
A tiger and a polar bear,
Lots of animals everywhere –
And I'm the king
So let us sing …

Chorus (x 2)

The song, the song (ooh la la) of the strong.
*(It's a jungle out there –
ROOOOAAARRR!)*

Animals

The lion song | Worksheet A

Write animal names. Listen, and play bingo!

Animal Bingo A

Animal Bingo B

A memory game | Worksheet B

Animals

jackal	snake	elephant	antelope	ant
shark	duck	crocodile	hippo	monkey
kangaroo	camel	mouse	mice	gnu
rabbit	frog	buffalo	tiger	polar bear

going to

14 The *going to* song

CD1 Track 20

Language focus	The *going to* form to express future time
Level	Post-beginners / A1
Time	Lesson 1: 20 minutes
	Lesson 2: about 30 minutes
Materials	CD1 – Track 20: audio recording of the song
	CD2/CD-ROM part: *The going to song* Flashcards
	Lesson 1: a copy of the lyrics for each student; a copy of Worksheet A per student
	Lesson 2: a copy of Worksheet B per two students

In class

Lesson 1

1. Teach or revise the following phrases using the flashcards provided: *climb trees, play football, ride a pony, swim, play tennis, skateboard, read a book, meet friends, buy something, skate (with roller-skates), build a sandcastle, watch TV.*

2. Show the phrases with the help of the flashcards. The students say the words.

3. Hand out a copy of Worksheet A to each student. Play the song twice and ask the students to listen carefully. Ask them to tick the pictures of the actions which they can hear in the song.

4. Then ask the students to say the numbers of the pictures they have ticked.

5. Hand out a copy of the lyrics. Ask them to read the lyrics. Then play the song and the students sing along.

Puchta/Gerngross/Holzmann/Devitt | Grammar Songs & Raps | © Helbling Languages

Answers Items ticked should be the following:

2. buy roller-skates
3. ride a pony
6. swim in the sea
7. skate
9. watch TV
10. meet friends
11. play football
12. read

Lesson 2

1. Stand in front of the class and hold up a copy of Worksheet B. Point at a boy and then a girl, saying, e.g.:

   At the weekend Simon is going to play ping pong.
   At the weekend Lucy is going to go shopping with her mum.

2. Write the two sentences on the board.

3. Tell your students to work in pairs, and hand Worksheet B to each pair.

4. Write on the board the sentence:

   What is … going to do at the weekend?

   Then explain the game to your students: both students look at the worksheet for a minute. Then A takes the worksheet so B cannot see it and asks the question: *What is … going to do at the weekend?* B tries to remember and say what the person is going to do. If B is right, she/he gets one point. Then B takes the worksheet and asks a question. Tell the students to take notes of the points each player achieves.

5. When each partner has asked ten questions they check who got the most points.

Extension

The students work in groups of four, and one asks what the others are going to do at the weekend. Then the interviewer reports back to the class.

The *going to* song

You're going to play football in the summer,
You're going to watch some TV,
You're going to ride on a pony,
You're going to swim in the sea.

But what am I going to do
In the summer, without you?
But what am I going to do
In the summer, without you?

You're going to Rome in the summer,
You're going to stay in Madrid,
You're going to San Francisco,
You're going to do that – that's it!

Chorus

I'm going to read lots of books,
I'm going to have lots of fun,
I'm going to meet with my friends,
In the summer, in the sun!

I'm going to buy roller-skates,
We're going to skate in the sun.
I'm going to meet all my mates,
We're going to have so much fun.

And that's what I'm going to do
In the summer, without you.
And that's what I'm going to do
In the summer, without you.
(repeat last stanza)

going to

The *going to* song | Worksheet A

Listen, look and tick ✓.

1. ☐
2. ☐
3. ☐
4. ☐
5. ☐
6. ☐
7. ☐
8. ☐
9. ☐
10. ☐
11. ☐
12. ☐

The *going to* song | Worksheet B

going to

Remember what they are going to do.

Simon	Lucy	Mark
Daisy	Oliver	Emma
Tom	Kate	Dylan
Pippa	Daniel	Lara

Puchta/Gerngross/Holzmann/Devitt | Grammar Songs & Raps | © Helbling Languages PHOTOCOPIABLE

Past tense

15 The Western star

CD2 Track 01

Language focus	Past tense for narration
Level	Elementary / A2 upwards
Time	Lesson 1: 20–30 minutes
	Lesson 2: (consecutive) 20–30 minutes
Materials	CD2 – Track 01: audio recording of the song
	CD2/CD-ROM part: *The Western star* Flashcard
	Lesson 1: a copy of the lyrics per pair of students; a copy of Worksheet A (cut up so each line of the song is on a strip of paper; put all the strips in an envelope)
	Lesson 2: a copy of Worksheet B per pair of students; a few pairs of scissors.

In class

Lesson 1

1. Show the students the cowboy flashcard.

   Write on the board the words *Western star* and ask students to call out words that come to mind. Write the words on the board so that it looks, for example, like this:

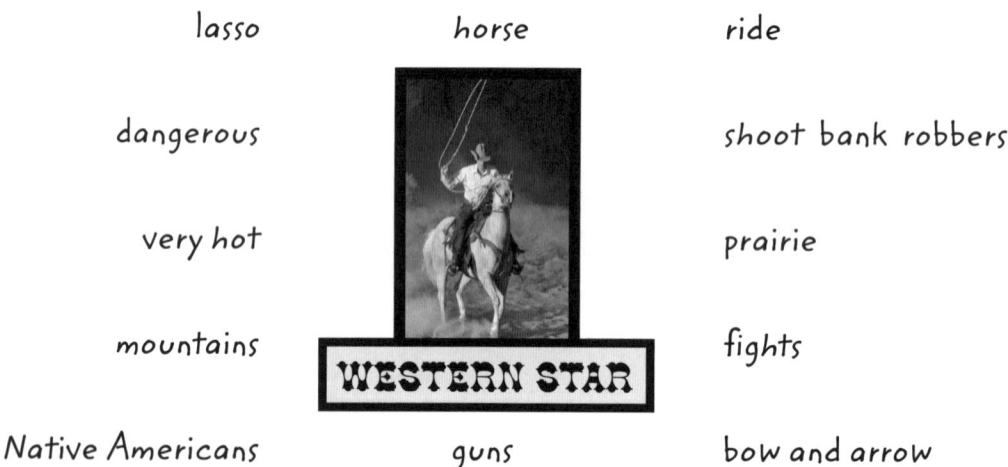

   lasso   horse   ride

   dangerous   shoot bank robbers

   very hot   prairie

   mountains   fights

   Native Americans   guns   bow and arrow

2. Write down these two headings and ask students to come up with suggestions. If necessary, give an example for each, e.g. as shown here:

   In Western films, cowboys …   **In reality, they …**
   fight all the time   had to work a lot.
   …   …

3. Hand out the lyrics strips you've prepared (see Note 3 on p. 74) and ask each student to read their line. At this stage make sure they understand the language. Now ask them to stand up and walk around the class trying to find students who have the line before or after their own. Let them know they have approximately three minutes to do this.

4. After three minutes, tell students to stop. Ask them to stand in a line, with the student who believes they have the first line of the song in front, the student who believes they have the second line standing next and so on. The student who believes they have the last line stands last in the line.

5. Ask students to read out the lyrics one by one, starting with the student in front. Tell students to read loudly and clearly.

6. Ask students what they think of the order. Most probably they will have noticed some incoherent points. Tell them that you will play the song now, and while listening they should adjust the order of the lines in the following way:

   - When a line is playing, the student who has the respective strip of paper has to hold their hand up as long as the line is playing.

   - If the student who is standing at the front of the queue has indeed the right strip of paper, they remain where they are. If another student (who is standing somewhere else in the row) has the first line, this student comes to the front and stands in first position now.

   - When the second line is playing, the student who has the respective strip of paper holds up their hand again, and moves to position 2 if they have been in a wrong position. The student stays where they are if already they are in the right position.

7. You may want to collect the strips and repeat the whole process from step 1 one more time.

8. Hand out a copy of the lyrics. Play the song again and get students to sing along.

Answer See Worksheet A.

Lesson 2

1. Give each pair of students a copy of Worksheet B. Get them to find pairs of pictures and write the corresponding letters in the bottom group.

2. Tell students to use *The clumsy cowboy wanted to… So he … but then …* and the phrases as prompts. Get them to match the sentence halves with the pictures, putting the verbs into past tense. Example:

   He wanted to go for a ride. So he got on his horse, but then he fell off.

3. Students read out their sentences, while you check that they've ended up with correctly matching pairs.

4. Tell students to study the sentences well and to test each other, taking turns to cover up the second picture in a pair with the other student trying to recall the sentences.

5. They then cut out the pictures and put them face down on the desk. Student A turns over a card, saying the sentence for it, e.g. *The cowboy wanted to enjoy an evening on the prairie.* Student B tries to say the follow-up sentence, i.e. *He sat down, but there was a cactus.* If the sentence is correct, Student B gets the card. Otherwise, A puts the card back on the desktop (face down), and the cards get shuffled again.

Past tense

If Student A draws a card with the second picture of a pair, Student B has to say the sentence that comes before, e.g. A: *So he got his guitar, but then he sat down on a cactus.* B: *He wanted to enjoy an evening on the prairie.*

The student who has the most cards in the end is the winner.

Answers

He wanted to go for a ride. So he got on his horse, but then he fell off.
The cowboy wanted to catch a wild horse. So he threw his lasso, but then he bumped his head against a tree.
He wanted to put the bank robbers in prison. So he went into the bank, but then he panicked when he saw a mouse.
He wanted to kiss a beautiful lady. So he bought her some flowers, but then he fell down the stairs.
He wanted to enjoy an evening on the prairie. So he got his guitar, but then he sat on a cactus.
He wanted to win the rodeo. So he chose a horse, but then he got scared and ran away.

Notes: Lesson 1

1. This activity is a lot of fun as it involves music and movement. At the same time, it's excellent for helping students to become aware of coherence in a text. They begin to notice how elements in a text hang together (e.g. grammatically, content-wise, through rhyming words etc.).

2. You may want to tell students that they have to move several times during the song if they have a line that is part of the chorus (these lines are in italics).

3. The worksheet is designed for 17 students. If you have fewer students in your class, you can either ask some students to take two strips of paper, or you can cut up the lyrics so that some students have two lines on their strip of paper rather than one. If there are more than 17 students, give some of the lines to pairs of students rather than individuals.

The Western star

I dreamed I was a Western star,
I rode the country high and far.
I never hung my hat for long,
I rode and whistled my sad song.

Riding, riding, riding,
Riding, riding all day long.
Wind and storm and weather,
Life's not getting better,
Riding, riding all day long.

One day, the sun was going down,
I came into a sleepy town,
I met a lovely lady there,
I fought and shot, and I won her.

Chorus

I kissed the lady, she kissed me,
Then I woke up. In front of me
My mother stood. "Now get up, son!"
So no more lady, horse and gun.

Chorus

The Western star | Worksheet A

Line up in order.

I dreamed I was a Western star,

I rode the country high and far.

I never hung my hat for long,

I rode and whistled my sad song.

One day, the sun was going down,

I came into a sleepy town,

I met a lovely lady there,

I fought and shot, and I won her.

I kissed the lady, she kissed me,

Then I woke up. In front of me

My mother stood: "Now get up, son!"

So no more lady, horse and gun.

Riding, riding, riding,

Riding, riding all day long.

Wind and storm and weather,

Life's not getting better,

Riding, riding all day long.

Past tense

The Clumsy Cowboy game | Worksheet B

With a partner, match each picture from the top group to one in the bottom group. Use the language to say what really happened to the clumsy cowboy. Use the past tense.

The clumsy cowboy wanted to…

kiss a beautiful lady	enjoy an evening on the prairie	catch a wild horse
win the rodeo	go for a ride	put the bank robbers in prison

So he … but then …

buy her some flowers / fall down the stairs	get on his horse / fall off	throw his lasso / bump his head against a tree
go into the bank / panic when he sees mouse	choose a horse / get scared and run away	get his guitar / sit on a cactus

16 The Gang of Four

Past tense

CD2 Track 02

Language focus	Past tense questions
Level	Elementary / A2
Time	Lesson 1: 20–30 minutes
	Lesson 2: (consecutive) 20–30 minutes
Materials	CD2 – Track 02: audio recording of the song
	Lesson 1: a copy of Worksheet A per student
	Lesson 2: copy Worksheet B, and produce a set of cards by cutting them out

In class

Lesson 1

1. Play the song. Tell students to listen, and try and remember as much language as possible. Tell them to call out words and phrases they remember, and write them on the board in random order.

2. Give each student a copy of Worksheet A. Get them to try and complete the lyrics by writing the respective number of the missing lines in pencil into the gaps.

3. Tell students to work with a partner and compare their choices. Then play the song again so students can check.

4. Play the song again. Get students to sing along.

Answer

3 Did Davey steal the jewels
8 Did Dinah steal the painting
11 It was the Gang of Four!
1 'Cause crime doesn't pay!
5 Did Harry do the bank job
9 Did Helen steal those handbags

2 Did Freddie take our wallets?
4 Did Fergie take all the gold coins?
6 To solve crime after crime.
7 To catch the Gang of Four.
10 Oh yeah, doesn't pay!

Lesson 2

1. Give each student a card from the Past Tense Questions Loop Game (Worksheet B). Ask your students to read their cards; also, make sure they know how to pronounce what's written on their card, and understand what it means. Get them to call you if they are unsure. If there are fewer than 21 students in your class, give 2 cards to some of the students. If there are more than 21, give some cards to pairs of students rather than individuals.

2. Tell the students that they are going to play a loop game. Make sure they know which of the sentences on their card is a question (Q) and which is an answer (A). Explain the game: one student starts the game by reading out the question on their card. The others have to listen carefully. Only one student has the correct answer to that question.

3. That student reads out the answer, and then continues by reading out the question on their card. The student who has got the answer to that question reads it out, and continues by reading out the question they have etc. The game

Past tense

   is called a loop game because if the game is played correctly, the student who starts the game is also the one who finishes it.

4. The game is over when all the questions and answers have been read, but it can be repeated many times. In this case, collect the cards and hand them out again in random order.

Answers

A: Yes, they did. They said it was very good.
Q: What did the men take from the house?
A: They took all the money, a watch, and some paintings.
Q: Did the police find the money?
A: Yes, they found it. It was in a hole in an old tree.
Q: Did Mike Hammer steal the old lady's handbag?
A: No, he didn't. Gordon Knife stole it.
Q: Did the police arrest the gang of robbers?
A: Yes, they did. They arrested them when they came out of the bank.
Q: Did Inspector Lime know who the robber was?
A: No he didn't, but he had a clever idea.
Q: Did the police find any fingerprints?
A: Yes, they did. There were fingerprints on the gun.
Q: Did the man break into the bank?
A: No, he didn't break into it. He had a key.
Q: Did the alarm go off when they came into the bank?
A: Yes, it did, and everybody could hear it.
Q: Did the thief keep all the money?
A: No, he didn't keep it. He lost it when he tried to run away.
Q: Did someone hear the robbers?
A: Nobody heard anything. They made no noise.
Q: How did the man in the car know that the robbers were coming?
A: He knew because the robbers told him. They had mobile phones.
Q: What did the people in the bank say after the robbery?
A: They didn't say much. They were all shocked.
Q: Who took the money out of the safe?
A: Nobody knows. The safe was locked.
Q: What did the bank manager say?
A: The bank manager? He was very angry.
Q: When did the men come into the bank?
A: At eight o'clock.
Q: Did you read what happened?
A: No, I didn't read about it. I saw it on TV.
Q: Where were you at 8 o'clock?
A: I was at home, listening to music.
Q: Did you break the vase?
A: No, I didn't. I think it was the cat.
Q: When did the inspector phone you?
A: He didn't phone. He came to my house.
Q: Did you like the detective film?
A: No, I didn't. I thought it was boring.
Q: Did your friends like the detective film?

Notes If you want to play loop game as a self-correcting game, tell your students the mechanics of the game, but when they make a mistake, don't tell them. In that case, the loop will not be complete. In other words, the student who has started the game will not finish it. Get students to play the game again (maybe several times) and watch very carefully to find out where things go wrong until they achieve a real loop.

See Puchta/Rinvolucri, *Multiple Intelligences in EFL*, p. 94 for more ideas on Loop Games.

The Gang of Four

Did Davey steal the jewels
When all the lights went out?
Did Dinah steal the painting
When no one was about?

*No, they didn't.
No, they didn't.
Someone stole more,
Someone stole more.
It was the Gang of Four!
And they won't get away –
'Cause crime doesn't pay!
Hey, hey, hey, hey,
Hey, hey, hey, hey.*

Did Harry do the bank job
On Thirty-seventh Street?
Did Helen steal those handbags
That were on the front seat?

Chorus

Did Freddie take our wallets?
Yes! Fred the master thief!
Did Fergie take all the gold coins?
Did she? Hard to believe!

Chorus

(Over there! Come out with your hands up!)

So now
It's up to Lime
To solve crime after crime.
To solve them – and what's more:
To catch the Gang of Four.
So they won't get away.
'Cause crime, 'cause crime, 'cause crime
Oh yeah, doesn't pay!

(You'd better believe it, boys and girls.)

Past tense
The Gang of Four | Worksheet A

Find the missing lines.

[ ]

When all the lights went out?

[ ]

When no one was about?

Chorus:
No, they didn't.
No, they didn't.
Someone stole more,
Someone stole more.

[ ]

And they won't get away –

[ ]

[ ]

On Thirty-seventh Street?

[ ]

That were on the front seat?

[ ]

Yes! Fred the master thief!

[ ]

Did she? Hard to believe!

So now
It's up to Lime

[ ]

To solve them – and what's more:

[ ]

So they won't get away.
'Cause crime, 'cause crime, 'cause crime

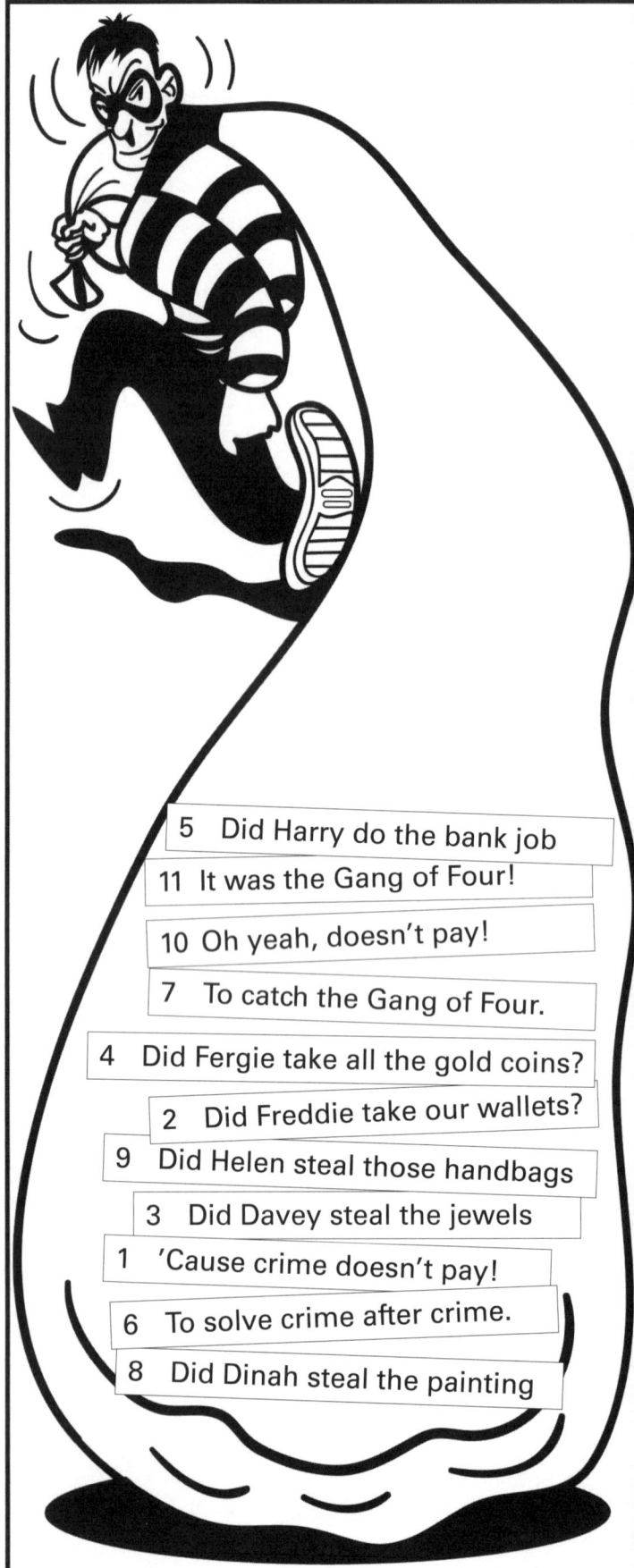

[ ]

5 Did Harry do the bank job
11 It was the Gang of Four!
10 Oh yeah, doesn't pay!
7 To catch the Gang of Four.
4 Did Fergie take all the gold coins?
2 Did Freddie take our wallets?
9 Did Helen steal those handbags
3 Did Davey steal the jewels
1 'Cause crime doesn't pay!
6 To solve crime after crime.
8 Did Dinah steal the painting

Past Tense Questions Loop Game | Worksheet B

A: They took all the money, a watch, and some paintings. Q: Did the police find the money?	A: Yes, they did. They arrested them when they came out of the bank. Q: Did Inspector Lime know who the robber was?	A: Yes, they did. There were fingerprints on the gun. Q: Did the man break into the bank?
A: Yes, it did, and everybody could hear it. Q: Did the thief keep all the money?	A: At eight o'clock. Q: Did you read what happened?	A: Yes, they found it. It was in a hole in an old tree. Q: Did Mike Hammer steal the old lady's handbag?
A: No, he didn't. Gordon Knife stole it. Q: Did the police arrest the gang of robbers?	A: They didn't say much. They were all shocked. Q: Who took the money out of the safe?	A: No, he didn't keep it. He lost it when he tried to run away. Q: Did someone hear the robbers?
A: No, he didn't break into it. He had a key. Q: Did the alarm go off when they came into the bank?	A: No, I didn't read about it. I saw it on TV. Q: Where were you at 8 o'clock?	A: No he didn't, but he had a clever idea. Q: Did the police find any fingerprints?
A: He knew because the robbers told him. They had mobile phones. Q: What did the people in the bank say after the robbery?	A: Nobody knows. The safe was locked. Q: What did the bank manager say?	A: Nobody heard anything. They made no noise. Q: How did the man in the car know that the robbers were coming?
A: The bank manager? He was very angry. Q: When did the men come into the bank?	A: No, I didn't. I think it was the cat. Q: When did the inspector phone you?	A: I was at home, listening to music. Q: Did you break the vase?
A: Yes, they did. They said it was very good. Q: What did the men take from the house?	A: He didn't phone. He came to my house. Q: Did you like the detective film?	A: No, I didn't. I thought it was boring. Q: Did your friends like the detective film?

Adjectives

17 The badbad beasts

CD2 Track 03

Language focus	Comparison of adjectives (superlatives)
Level	Elementary / A2
Time	Lesson 1: 15 minutes
	Lesson 2: 15 minutes
Materials	CD2 – Track 03: audio recording of the song
	CD2/CD-ROM part: *The badbad beasts* Flashcard
	Lesson 1: a copy of Worksheet A per student
	Lesson 2: one copy of Worksheets B and C per group of three students; have a dice and a pair of scissors for each group of three, and have enough sets of three different tokens (e.g. red, yellow and blue plastic counters, or paper clips, buttons and erasers) for each student to have one token.

In class

Lesson 1

1. Hold up a picture of an unusual animal/beast, such as the flashcard below.

   Ask students to give you adjectives that go with the picture. Collect them on the board. Some students might want to add an adjective which they haven't learned yet. Encourage them to say: *What's … in English?* Practise the pronunciation of the new words.

2. Tell them the animal in the picture lived on Earth millions of years ago. It wasn't just big, but *the biggest!* Ask students to form the superlative of the other adjectives on the board. If necessary, revise how to form superlatives.

3. Play the song. Ask them if they can remember any of the adjectives that describe each of the beasts mentioned in the song. List the words they can remember on the board.

Adjectives

4. Hand out Worksheet A. Play the song again if necessary and ask students to do the first task (matching) and compare their answers in pairs.

5. Then ask the students to think of two adjectives each for the other four animals mentioned in the song. Ask them to find the superlatives for these words. Then ask individual students to read out their adjectives in the superlative.

6. Ask them to draw one of the animals for homework and write the superlatives that go with it underneath the picture. Display the pictures in class.

Answers

Snapkle	biggest
Ruckle	best
Bugboy	most dangerous
Bombom	loudest
Bombom	angriest
Bombom	most stupid
Googler	meanest
Googler	wildest
Googler	most intelligent

Lesson 2

1. Play the song again. Ask the students to pay special attention to the adjectives.

2. Hand out Worksheet B. Explain the board game to the students:

Get together in groups of three. You're going to play a game. Each group will get a board for the game, a dice, and three tokens. Each group will also get a worksheet with cards. Please cut out the cards. Then shuffle them and put them face down next to the board.

Give your students enough time to prepare for the game.

3. Explain to your class how the game works. Tell them that each group has to decide who goes first. Then students throw the dice and move their tokens etc. Tell them that if they land on a grey square, they have to pick up a card and follow the instructions. They take turns throwing the dice. The first one to get to Atlantis is the winner.

Extension

Students can make up their own cards and even their own beasts; in other words they can make up a new version of the game. Ask them to come up with new names for beasts from Atlantis. Collect the names on the board and assign each group of three a few names. Then ask them to come up with adjectives in their groups. They can make their own cards, computer-generated or handwritten, using the model on Worksheet C. Then ask them to play their own version of the game.

Adjectives

The badbad beasts

Uh huh huh, yeah yeah –
Uh huh huh, yeah yeah –

The Snapkle was the biggest,
The Ruckle was the best,
The Bugboy the most dangerous –
But what about the rest?

Hey people, shout it out, shout it out!
Yeah, and what about –

The Rippety and the Rappety?
The Lickety and the Lackety?
And all the other badbad beasts
That came to all Atlantean feasts?

Uh huh huh, yeah yeah –
Uh huh huh, yeah yeah –

The Bombom was the loudest,
It was the angriest too,
And some say the most stupid –
He couldn't count to two.

Hey people, shout it out, shout it out!
Yeah, and what about –

Chorus

Uh huh huh, yeah yeah –
Uh huh huh, yeah yeah –

The Googler was the meanest,
The wildest in a fight
And (yes!) the most intelligent,
He hunted every night.

Hey people, shout it out, shout it out!
Yeah, and what about –

Chorus

They all sunk with Atlantis.
That was the saddest day
For all the badbad beasties –
They're gone. Hooray! Hooray!

One, two, a-one, two, three four –
They're gone. Hooray! Hooray!
(repeat quickly)

(Thank you very much, uh huh huh.)

The badbad beasts | Worksheet A

1 Listen to the song and draw lines to match the words on the right with the pictures of the five beasts. Some beasts have more than one word.

1 Snapkle
2 Ruckle
3 Bugboy
4 Bombom
5 Googler

- best
- most stupid
- biggest
- angriest
- wildest
- most intelligent
- loudest
- most dangerous
- meanest

2 Now think of adjectives that could go with the Rippety, the Rappety, the Lickety and the Lackety. Write down two adjectives for each beast. Use the superlative.

Rippety _____ _____

Rappety _____ _____

Lickety _____ _____

Lackety _____ _____

Adjectives

The beasts game | Worksheet B

Get together in groups of three. Cut out the cards on worksheet C and put them face down on your desk.

Use the board and dice. Each of you has a token. Take turns throwing the dice. Whenever your token lands on a dark grey square, pick up a card and read the instructions. The first one to get to Atlantis is the winner.

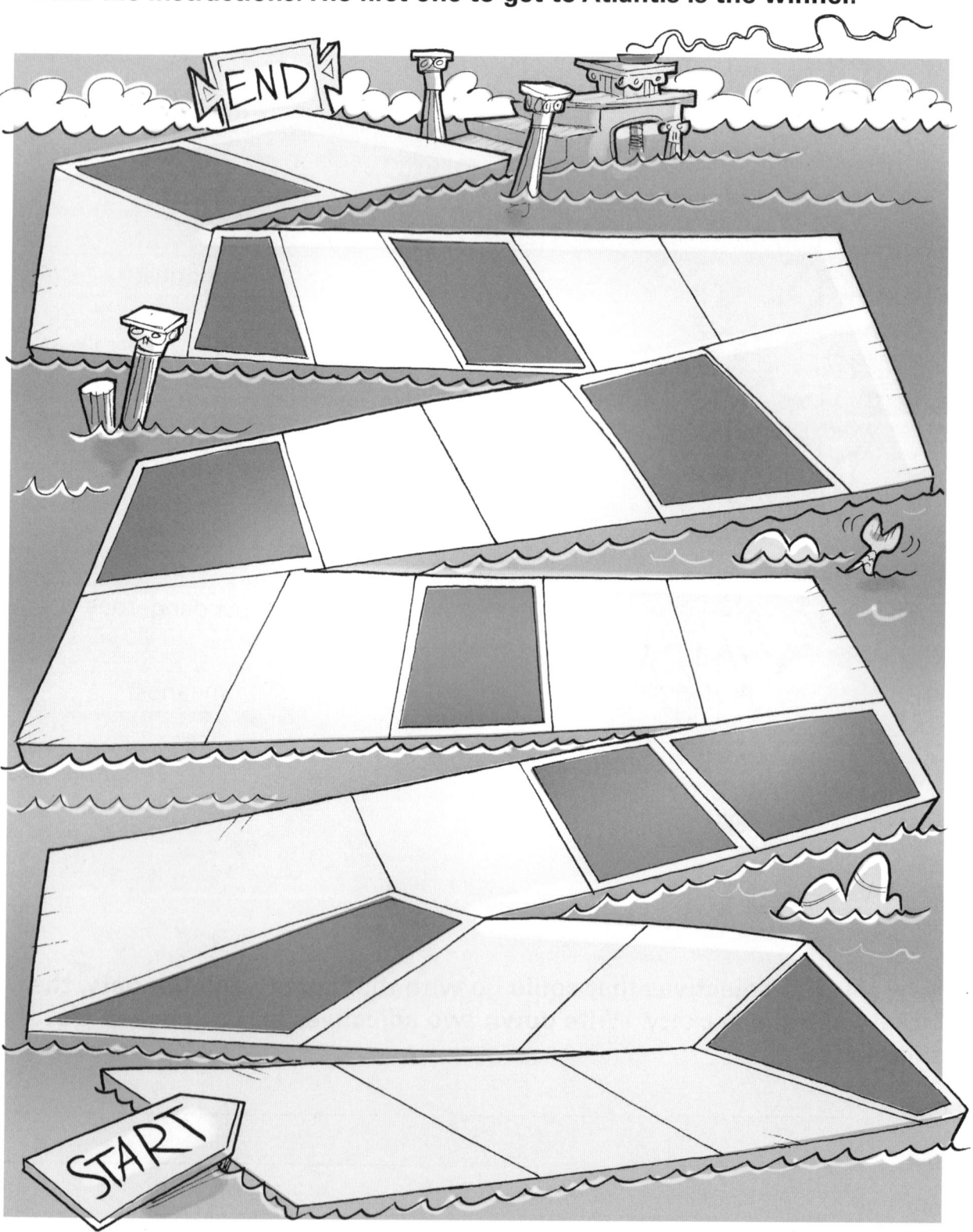

The badbad beasts | Worksheet C

Adjectives

STOP! The meanest beast is watching you. Which one is it? If you can name it, have another turn. If not, go back two steps.

STOP! The most dangerous beast is watching you. Which one is it? If you can name it, have another turn. If not, go back three steps.

STOP! The most intelligent beast is watching you. Which one is it? If you can name it, have another turn. If not, go back four steps.

STOP! The biggest beast is watching you. Which one is it? If you can name it, have another turn. If not, go back two steps.

STOP! The best beast is watching you. Which one is it? If you can name it, have another turn. If not, go back one step.

STOP! The loudest beast is watching you. Which one is it? If you can name it, have another turn. If not, go back two steps.

STOP! The angriest beast is watching you. Which one is it? If you can name it, have another turn. If not, go back three steps.

STOP! The most stupid beast is watching you. Which one is it? If you can name it, have another turn. If not, go back four steps.

STOP! The wildest beast is watching you. Which one is it? If you can name it, have another turn. If not, go back three steps.

STOP! The Rippety is coming. Go back five steps to get away from it.

STOP! You see the Rappety eating wild flowers. Quickly go forward two steps.

STOP! You see the Lickety and the Lackety fighting each other. Quickly go forward three steps.

have to

18 All my *have-tos*
a rap

CD2 Track 04/05

Language focus	*have to*
Level	Elementary / A2
Time	Lesson 1: 20 minutes
	Lesson 2: 20 minutes
Materials	CD2 – Track 04: audio recording of the rap
	CD2 – Track 05: karaoke version of the rap
	Lesson 1: a copy of the lyrics for each student; a copy of Worksheet A per student
	Lesson 2: a copy of Worksheet B per group of four students. Bring scissors for each group. Prepare a slide with Worksheet C or use the *Have-to* ppt provided in the CD-ROM part of CD 2. Use different scores to repeat the game.

In class

Lesson 1

1. Tell students one or two things you *have to* do today. For example: *I have to teach four more lessons today. I have to repair my bike today.* Then ask: *What about you?* Ask individual students what they have to do that day. Write verb phrases on the board while students are talking, e.g.:

   study for a test
   help my mum/dad
   walk the dog
   tidy up my room
   write some emails

2. Students work in pairs and tell each other three things they have to do today/tomorrow. If your class is not ready for that, it might be a good idea to present some more verb phrases, write them on the board and practise their pronunciation so students can use them with ease.

3. Hand out Worksheet A. Play the rap. Students do the first task, in which they tick the activities mentioned in the rap. Check in class.

4. Hand out the lyrics. Play the rap again and ask students to join in.

5. Then students do the second task, in which they write twelve sentences that go with the pictures. They compare the results in pairs.

Answers These activities should be ticked:

do your homework	get some sleep	get new clothes	do the dishes	play football
cut the grass	take exams	run a race	do your push-ups	

Lesson 2

1. Play the rap and revise what the people in it *have to* do. Ask individual students if they can name at least two examples from the rap. Ask them if they ever have to do these things, for example: *Do you ever have to cut the grass?*

2. Hand out Worksheet B. Explain the game to the students and put them into groups of four. Tell them that each student is going to get six cards and that each activity on this card is worth a certain number of points. Tell them that they have to swap cards with each other in their group, each student trying to end up with as high a score as possible. Tell them they will need to remember the scores you will show them. Then display to the students the slide for 30 seconds. Those who memorise the points of the activities best will probably win.

3. Stop the activity after five minutes and ask students to add up their scores.

4. Ask each group to announce its winner.

Extension

If the students are familiar with the game *Simon Says*, you can adapt it by using *have to* commands instead of simple commands. (In the original game, only the orders that are preceded by 'Simon says' are valid. If whoever's giving the orders commands an activity without the preceding 'Simon says' and you do the action, you are out of the game.) So for example, using *have to*:

Say: *Simon says you have to stand on one leg.* Everybody should stand on one leg.
Say: *You have to sit down.* Nobody should sit down, since 'Simon says' is missing. Anyone who sits down is out of the game.

Use the karaoke version as suggested on pp. 7-8.

All my *have-tos*

You have to do your homework,
You have to get some sleep,
You have to get some new clothes,
You have to get them cheap.

But you don't have to love it! (Uh-uh)
But you don't have to love it! (Uh-uh)
But you don't have to love it at all! (Uh-uh)

You have to do the dishes,
You have to cut the grass,
You have to take exams, and
You have to, have to pass.

Chorus

There are a million things you have to do,
You have to do each day.
If you don't want to do them –
You have to go away.
Away, away, you have to go away.

You have to go play football,
You have to run a race,
You have to do your push-ups,
You have to stay in place.

You have to do your homework,
You have to get some sleep,
You have to get some new clothes,
You have to get them cheap.

You have to do the dishes,
You have to cut the grass,
You have to take exams, and
You have to, have to pass.

Or do you have to?
Or do you have to?

have to

All my *have-tos* | Worksheet A

Listen to the rap and tick ✓ the activities you hear.

Now write a sentence for each picture, e.g:

He/She has to do the dishes.

The *have-to* game | Worksheet B

Get together in groups of four. Cut out one set of cards. Each of you gets six cards. The teacher will show you briefly how many points you can get for each thing you have to do.

Look at your cards, and decide which ones you don't want (because you think they have a low score). Try to swap with your partners. You have got 5 minutes for swapping.

At the end, your teacher will show you again the number of points for each task. Add up your points. The one with most points is the winner.

Example:
A: I have to do the dishes. Who wants to swap with me?
B: OK. I have to get some rest after school. I'm happy to swap. Here you are.

have to do my homework in the afternoon	have to do the dishes in the evening	have to meet my friend at 12:30
have to get some sleep today	have to buy some clothes in the afternoon	have to read two books by Sunday
have to cut the grass in the morning	have to take an exam at four	have to help Dad in the kitchen when he comes home
have to play football from five to six	have to run a race at 11 o'clock	have to fill in two worksheets in my break
have to do push-ups first thing in the morning	have to play volleyball in the third lesson	have to be home by eight today
have to make the bed when I get up	have to paint my room in the afternoon	have to clean my bike right now
have to help with the cooking at lunchtime	have to get some rest after school	have to be at the bus stop in 5 minutes
have to watch a DVD in the evening	have to check my emails right away	have to phone my mum in half an hour

have to

All my *have-tos* | Worksheet C

Write a score from 1 to 4 in each of the boxes.

☐	have to do my homework in the afternoon	☐	have to do the dishes in the evening
☐	have to get some sleep today	☐	have to buy some clothes in the afternoon
☐	have to cut the grass in the morning	☐	have to take an exam at four
☐	have to play football from five to six	☐	have to run a race at 11 o'clock
☐	have to do push-ups first thing in the morning	☐	have to play volleyball in the third lesson
☐	have to make the bed when I get up	☐	have to paint my room in the afternoon
☐	have to help with the cooking at lunchtime	☐	have to get some rest after school
☐	have to watch a DVD in the evening	☐	have to check my emails right away
☐	have to meet my friend at 12:30	☐	have to be home by eight today
☐	have to read two books by Sunday	☐	have to clean my bike right now
☐	have to help Dad in the kitchen when he comes home	☐	have to be at the bus stop in 5 minutes
☐	have to fill in two worksheets in my break	☐	have to phone my mum in half an hour

19 I'm not going to ...

not going to

CD2 Track 06

Language focus	not going to
Level	Elementary / A2
Time	Lesson 1: 20 minutes
	Lesson 2: 20 minutes
Materials	CD2 – Track 06: audio recording of the song
	Lesson 1: a copy of Worksheet A per student
	Lesson 2: a copy of the lyrics for each student; pepare a cardboard copy of Worksheet B per pair. Ask the students to bring scissors.

In class

Lesson 1

1. Ask your students a few specific questions about what they are going to do after school, e.g: *Are you going to watch a DVD today?* Expect short answers.

2. Tell them one or two things you are definitely **not** going to do within the next few days.

3. Ask them to get together in pairs and tell each other a few things they are not going to do within the next few days, e.g.:

   A: I'm not going to do the dishes today.
   B: Right. And I'm not going to tidy the living room today.

   Check some of the sentences by asking a student what his/her partner is not going to do.

4. Hand out Worksheet A and ask the students to listen and write a sentence about the activities the singer is not going to do underneath each picture. Three activities are not mentioned in the song. Tell them to put an X next to those pictures. Then play the song.

5. Check the answers in class.

Answer   Sentences should be written for:
The boy isn't going to write a letter.
The boy isn't going to send a mail.
The boy isn't going to sit here and wail.
The boy isn't going to text.
The boy isn't going to answer the phone.
The boy isn't going to cry.
The boy isn't going to say I love you.
There are 3 extra pictures: the boy buying flowers, the boy giving a present, the boy and girl holding hands.

Lesson 2

1. Hand out the lyrics, then play the song again. Ask the boys to sing along with the boy, and the girls to sing along with the girl.

Puchta/Gerngross/Holzmann/Devitt | Grammar Songs & Raps | © Helbling Languages

not going to

2. Hand out Worksheet B. Ask the students to get together in pairs and cut out the 30 domino cards. Tell them that each of them should take six dominoes. The rest are put in a stack face down on the desk between them.

   Student A starts by putting down one of his/her dominoes face up on the desk. If B has got a domino matching the sentence, he/she puts it down. If he/she can follow with another domino, he/she does so as many times as he/she can. When B can't play, he/she picks a domino from the stack and it is A's turn again (who plays as B did).

   Number cards: if either student puts down a domino with a number on it, they say any sentence with *not going to* that they can think of. When the matching number is put down, the student repeats the sentence as he/she puts down their card, and then the game continues as usual.

3. Students play the game. Whoever gets rid of their dominoes first is the winner.

   Extension 1

   Students could come up with a new version of the game by writing their own domino pieces. Or they could add as many as they like to the existing game.

   Extension 2

   Have them play again, but in groups of four.

I'm not going to ...

I'm not going to write you a letter,
I'm not going to send you a mail,
I'm not going to get any better,
But I'm not going to sit here and wail.

I'm not going to text you, you know,
I'm not going to answer the phone,
I'm not going to cry to show you
That I'm not going to feel good alone.

I'm not going to wait for replies,
I'm not going to say that we're through,
I'm not going to tell any lies.
I'm not going to say – I love you.

No, I'm not going to say – I love you.
I love you,
No, I'm not going to say – I love you.

I'm not going to ... | Worksheet A

Listen to the song. Write the correct sentences next to the pictures that show activities from the song. There are three extra pictures.

Example: The boy isn't going to write a letter.

Puchta/Gerngross/Holzmann/Devitt | Grammar Songs & Raps | © Helbling Languages **PHOTOCOPIABLE**

not going to

The *not going to* dominoes game | Worksheet B

Play in pairs. Cut out the domino pieces. Shuffle them and put them face down. Each of you picks 6 pieces, then pile the rest on the desk face down.

Play dominoes to find the matching pairs. For each piece with a number, make up a sentence with **not going to**. If your partner has got a piece with the same number, he/she repeats the sentence while putting the card down.

I'm not going to write you a letter.	1
I'm not going to wait for replies.	I'm not going to send you an email.
I'm not going to sit here.	I'm not going to buy you some flowers.
2	3
I'm not going to feel good.	I'm not going to wail.
4	I'm not going to cry.
I'm not going to text you.	I'm not going to say I love you.
I'm not going to buy you CDs.	I'm not going to answer the phone.
5	I'm not going to say goodbye.
I'm not going to phone you at 8.	I'm not going to run after you.
I'm not going to come to your party.	6
7	8
I'm not going to get any better.	I'm not going to dream of you.
I'm not going to tell any lies.	And my friend isn't going to meet you.
9	And my friend isn't going to talk to you.

1	I'm not going to wait for replies.
I'm not going to send you an email.	I'm not going to sit here.
I'm not going to buy you some flowers.	2
I'm not going to wail.	3
I'm not going to cry.	I'm not going to feel good.
I'm not going to say I love you.	4
I'm not going to answer the phone.	I'm not going to text you.
I'm not going to buy you CDs.	5
I'm not going to run after you.	I'm not going to say goodbye.
6	I'm not going to phone you at 8.
I'm not going to come to your party.	7
8	I'm not going to get any better.
I'm not going to dream of you.	I'm not going to tell any lies.
And my friend isn't going to meet you.	9
And my friend isn't going to talk to you.	I'm not going to write you a letter.

20 The *some* and *any* rap

some, any

CD2 Track 07/08

Language focus	*Some, any*
Level	Elementary / A2
Time	Lesson 1: 20 minutes
	Lesson 2: 20 minutes
Materials	CD2 – Track 07: audio recording of the rap
	CD2 – Track 08: karaoke version of the rap
	CD2/CD-ROM part: *The some and any rap* Flashcards
	Lesson 1: a copy of Worksheet A per student
	Lesson 2: a copy of the lyrics for each student; a copy of Worksheet B per group of four. Ask them to bring scissors, and bring some spares yourself.

In class

Lesson 1:

1. Revise vocabulary for fruit and vegetables using the flashcards provided. Ask the students to shout out words they know and list them on the board.

2. Tell the students you are going to make some fruit salad. Ask them what kind of fruit they would want for it. Elicit answers like: *We/I want some oranges*, etc.

3. Tell the students you want to make a vegetable stew. Hand out your pictures of vegetables. Tell the students you need some carrots etc; e.g.: *Have you got any carrots for me?* Elicit replies like *Sorry, I haven't got any.* If somebody gives you a picture with carrots, say *thank you*.

4. Hand out Worksheet A and play the rap. Tell the students to write a tick ✓ for *some* or a cross ✗ for *any*.

5. Check the answers in class.

Answer

Puchta/Gerngross/Holzmann/Devitt | Grammar Songs & Raps | © Helbling Languages

some, any

Lesson 2

1. Play the rap. Then repeat it, with one group of students taking Pete's part, and one Andy's part. They all join in the chorus together.

2. Ask the students to get together in groups of four.

3. For each group, hand out a copy of Worksheet B. Introduce words that are new for your class with the help of the flashcards provided. Ask them to cut out the cards and to shuffle them. Each student gets six cards. If they have a set of four different fruit/vegetables they put the set aside right away.

4. Then the students play the game by asking each other for cards to get a set of four different fruit or vegetables. Student A starts, by saying, e.g.: *(Name of student), have you got any carrots for me?* Or: *Can I have some carrots from you, B?* If the answer is *Yes*, B gives A the card, and A may ask another question. If the answer is *No*, then it's B's turn to ask a question. Whoever gets the most sets is the winner.

5. Hand the winner of each group a strawberry or a grape or a carrot.

Note If you want to make the game longer and more challenging, prepare two sets for each group. This means everybody gets 12 cards and they really have to look out for four different items. Note that, e.g., bananas, bananas, oranges and apples do not make a set.

Extension

Students could come up with their own version of the game including *some* and *any* and a range of objects of their choice they can group under a heading, e.g.: *animals, school things, clothes.*

Use the karaoke version as suggested on pp. 7-8.

some, any

The *some* and *any* rap

(Pete,
Yes, Andy?
I really want to eat some fruit.
You really want to eat some fruit?
Yes. Look in the fridge, will you?)

Are there any peaches?
And are there any cherries?
I need them for my salad.
I also need some berries.

All these fruits fruits fruits
Are so good, good, good
All these fruits fruits fruits
Are so good, good, good
Mmmmm, mmmmm.

I'm sorry, oh so sorry,
We've got some beans, some carrots –
We haven't got any berries,
We haven't got any cherries.

Chorus

Whoa!
Are there any apples?
Or any kiwi fruit?
Are there any nuts?
Yeah, nuts would be so good.
Are there any grapes?
I'd love a juicy bunch.
I want to make a fruit salad
And eat it for my lunch.

I'm sorry, oh so sorry,
We've got some onions – oh
And also some tomatoes
But fruit? So sorry, no!

(We've only got some vegetables.)

We've got no fruit, fruit, fruit.
That's not so good, good, good.
(repeat x 4)
Oh no, oh no.

(Let's have some ice cream then. Oh yes!)

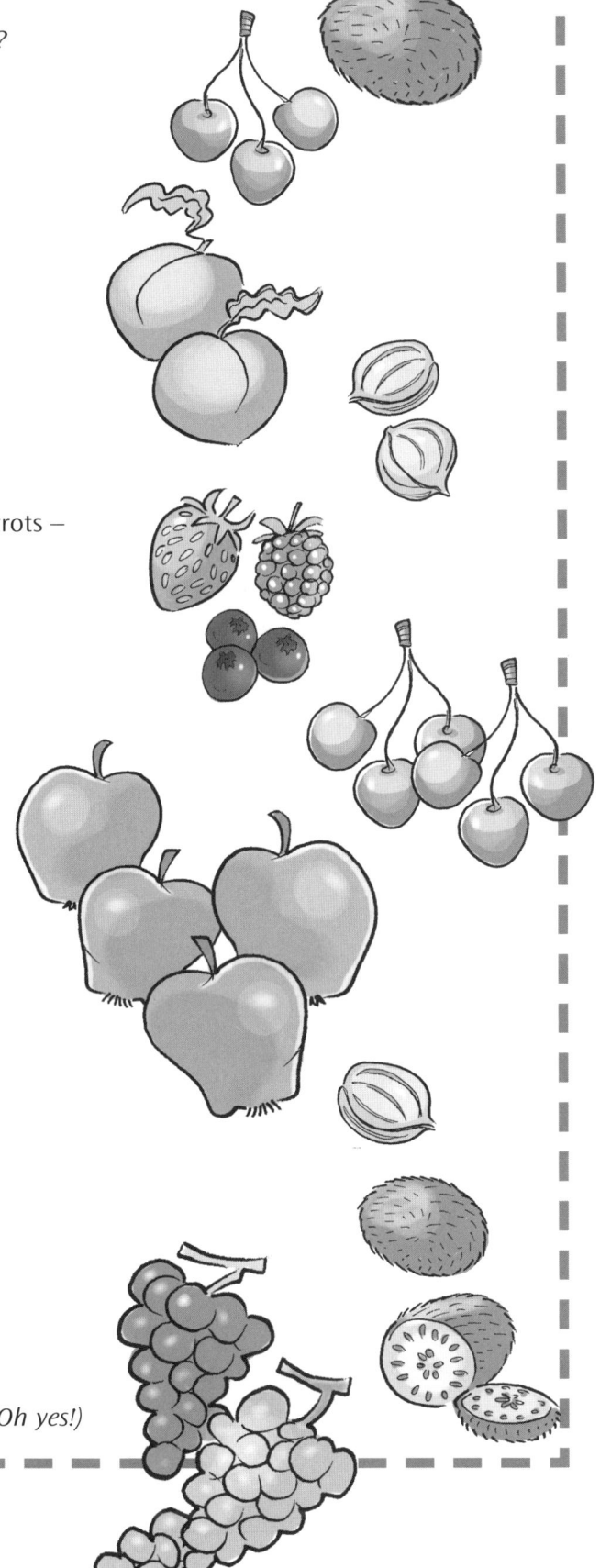

Puchta/Gerngross/Holzmann/Devitt | Grammar Songs & Raps | © Helbling Languages **PHOTOCOPIABLE**

some, any

What have(n't) they got? | Worksheet A

Look at the pictures. Then listen to the song and write a tick ✓ if there are *some*, or a cross ✗ if there aren't *any*. Check your answers with a partner.

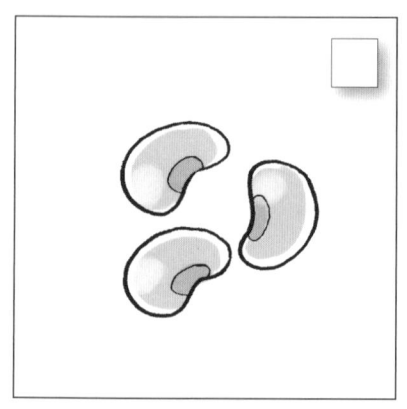

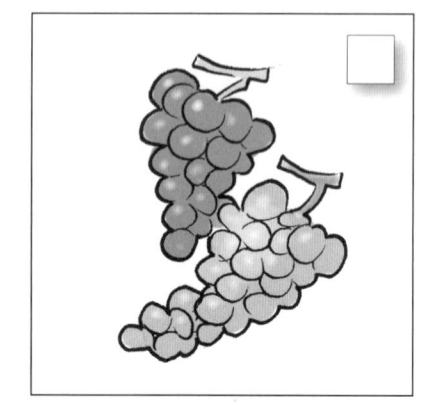

some, any

The fruit and vegetable game | Worksheet B

Cut out the cards for the game. Play in groups of four. You can make either a fruit salad (get four fruit cards) or a vegetable stew (get four vegetable cards). Take turns asking for cards.

For example, ask: *Can I have some berries?*
Answer: *Sorry, I haven't got any.* Or: *Here you are.*

Puchta/Gerngross/Holzmann/Devitt | Grammar Songs & Raps | © Helbling Languages **PHOTOCOPIABLE**

Past tense

21 The pyramids

CD2 Track 09

Language focus	Past tense
Level	Elementary / A2
Time	Lesson 1: 20 minutes
	Lesson 2: 20 minutes
Materials	CD2 – Track 09: audio recording of the song
	Lesson 1: a copy of Worksheet A per student
	Lesson 2: make a copy of the lyrics for each student; one copy of Worksheet B per group. Prepare copies of the game board. Prepare a list of names of the students and copy it for each group. Ask the students to bring dice and playing tokens. Bring a supply of scissors, one pair for each group.

In class

Lesson 1

1. Write *Ancient Egypt* on the board and draw a pyramid next to it. Ask the students if they know any words that go with ancient Egypt. Elicit the following words: *pyramid, Pharaoh, curse, evil, tomb* (plus *River Nile* and *mummy* if you wish, but they are not needed for the activities). If they do not know any of the words, teach them by using simple drawings.

2. Hand out Worksheet A and ask the students to guess the words for the pictures.

3. Play the song and ask the students to check whether they were right or not. If necessary, play the song again so they can fill in the correct words.

4. Ask them to check the answers in pairs.

5. Ask the students to do the second part of the worksheet. Remind them to use the past forms. Check the answers in class.

6. Have them draw a picture of what they saw. Then collect the pictures and put them up in class. Ask individual students for positive feedback. Students say: *I like the picture of the … because…*

Answers
1. kid, pyramid, went down, moon, scared, Pharaoh x 2, curse, nights
2. went, was, was, went, hid, tried, came, opened, fell, switched, saw

Lesson 2

1. Hand out the full lyrics. Play the song again and encourage the students to sing along (especially with the chorus).

2. Ask the students to form groups of 3–4. Hand out the game board and Worksheet B to each group. Ask students to cut out the cards and put them face down next to the game board.

3. Hand out a list of names to each group where students can enter their scores.

Past tense

4. Each student puts their tokens on START. Tell the students that each of them has got ten points to begin with. Student A throws the dice and moves along the squares etc. Whoever gets to a grey square has to pick up a card and read it out to the group. Then he/she has to add or take off points according to what the card says. Each student keeps track of their scores. (Theoretically they can finish the game with 10 points if they never land on a grey square.)

Extension

Students could come up with a new version of the game. They use the cards as models for new cards (e.g. 12 cards) they write in their groups. Then they swap their cards with the cards from another group and play the game again.

The pyramids

Well, there was this kid
And you know what he did?
One day he hid
In a pyramid.

When the sun went down
And the moon came up,
The kid was so scared
But no one really cared.

With a hey and a ho, and a hey and a ho
There's the mighty Pharaoh!
With a hey and a ho, and a hey and a ho
There's the mighty Pharaoh!
And his evil curse
Really makes things worse.

It's too bad, my friend.
Therefore never spend
Nights in pyramids!
They're not for kids.

Yeah, the pyramids,
They're not for kids.
No, they're not for kids.
Not the pyramids!

Chorus (x 2)

Yeah, the pyramids,
They're not for kids.
No, they're not for kids.
Not the pyramids!
(repeat x 2)

Well there was this kid
(There was this kid)
And you know what he did?
(Know what he did?)
One day he hid
(One day he hid)
In a pyramid.
(In a pyramid.)

When the sun went down
(Sun went down)
And the moon came up
(Moon came up),
The kid was so scared
But no one really cared.

Chorus

Puchta/Gerngross/Holzmann/Devitt | Grammar Songs & Raps | © Helbling Languages

Past tense

The pyramids | Worksheet A

1 Look at the text. Write the words under the pictures. Then listen to the song and check.

Well there was this _____

And you know what he did?
One day he hid

In a _____ .

When the sun _____

And the _____ came up,

The kid was so _____

But no one really cared.

With a hey and a ho, and a hey and a ho

There's the mighty _____ !

With a hey and a ho, and a hey and a ho

There's the mighty _____ !

And his evil _____

Really makes things worse.

It's too bad, my friend.
Therefore never spend

_____ in pyramids!

They're not for kids.

2 Fill in the past forms. Then draw what the kids saw. Check with a partner.

One night, my friend and I _____ (go) into a pyramid. I _____ (be) really scared but my friend _____ (be) not. When the sun _____ (go) down, we _____ (hide) in the pyramid. Then we _____ (try) to find the the Pharaoh's tomb. We _____ (come) to an old wooden door in the floor. We _____ (open) it. Everything was very dark and suddenly we _____ (fall) down the stairs under the door. My friend had a little torch with him. He _____ (switch) it on, and suddenly we _____ (see):

Past tense

The pyramid game | Worksheet B

Play the pyramid game in groups of 3–4. Get a token and throw the dice. Whenever you get to a grey square, pick a card. Read it out to your group and keep track of your score.

Everybody starts with ten points. The winner is the one who has the most points left when he/she gets to the top. (The score can be positive or negative.)

You have broken through the door into the pyramid. Get 3 points.	You forgot to bring a torch. Lose 2 points.
The moon came up an hour ago, but you can't see it. Lose 3 points.	You finally found the secret doorway. Get 4 points.
You heard somebody shout an evil curse. Lose 2 points.	You ran along a corridor for five minutes. Get 2 points.
Things just got worse – someone is after you! Lose 5 points.	You found a box of matches. Get 4 points.
You think you saw an evil face! Lose 2 points.	You heard a scream, but ignored it. Get 3 points.
You think you just saw the evil Pharaoh! Lose 2 points.	Somebody was after you. But you hid in a corner! Get 3 points.
You found a map. Get 2 points.	You noticed that your map is all wrong. Lose 3 points.
Suddenly you were totally scared. Lose 2 points.	You remembered you had a mobile phone in your bag. Get 1 point.
You just heard the Pharaoh is coming after you! Lose 2 points.	The Pharaoh caught your friend a minute ago. Lose all your points.

Puchta/Gerngross/Holzmann/Devitt | Grammar Songs & Raps | © Helbling Languages **PHOTOCOPIABLE**

Past tense

22 We are the ghosts

Tag questions

CD2 Track 10

Language focus	Tag questions
Level	Elementary / A2
Time	Lesson 1: 20 minutes Lesson 2: 20 minutes
Materials	CD2 – Track 10: audio recording of the song Lesson 1: prepare a copy of Worksheet A per student Lesson 2: make a copy of the lyrics for each student; prepare one copy of Worksheet B per group. Ask students to bring scissors, a pair for each group. Prepare a list to enter winner names.

In class

Lesson 1: What ghosts do

1. Write the word GHOSTS on the board, and brainstorm it for two minutes – i.e. let the students come up with whatever words they feel go with it. If necessary revise or teach *scare people, rattle chains, scream, castle*.

2. Hand out Worksheet A and play the song. Tell the students to cross out the things that were **not** mentioned in the song.

3. Check the answers to the first question in class.

4. Revise or introduce tag questions: Write a few examples on the board:

   There's a ghost in the castle, isn't there?
   The kids aren't afraid of ghosts, are they?
   Ghosts scare people, don't they?

5. Discuss question 2 in class.

6. Ask students to answer question 3 on the worksheet, and check the answers in class.

Answers
1 Things to be crossed out:
  break windows, climb down castle walls, wake everybody, laugh madly, fall asleep, dress in black
2 don't they, can't they, do they, are they

Lesson 2: A game for ghosts

1. Revise the vocabulary from Lesson 1. Use the phrases from Worksheet A; say, e.g., *rattle* and students complete the phrase by calling out *chains*; say *dress* and students call out *in sheets* etc.

2. Hand out the lyrics and play the song again. Ask them to sing along (with an extra group for the chorus).

Puchta/Gerngross/Holzmann/Devitt | Grammar Songs & Raps | © Helbling Languages

Tag questions

3. Hand out Worksheet B. Tell the students to cut up the worksheet and spread out the cards face down on their desks.

4. One student in the group starts the activity by picking up a card and miming the action for the others/their partner. If it is something ghosts do not do in the song, they indicate it at the beginning by an appropriate gesture for NO. The others try to guess the activity. Give a time-frame of 30 seconds for each guess. Emphasize that they really have to try and guess as quickly as possible. If they can't guess the action, the student puts the card back face down and shuffles the cards around a bit.

5. If the students guess correctly, the student who mimed the action can keep the card. The next student continues. If a student should pick up the same action-card in another round (since there are two for each activity), he/she has got a pair and gets two points. In this case there is no further miming and guessing for that card.

6. Enter the winners of each group on your list.

Extension

Ask your students to draw pictures of ghosts. Collect the pictures and put them up on the wall. Add some of your own if you wish. Ask students to get together in pairs; each student picks a ghost. Then they write a silent dialogue (see below) between the two ghosts. Ask them to come up with at least 12 sentences. Then ask a few pairs to read out their dialogues.

For a silent dialogue, Student A writes an opening sentence (e.g. *I look pretty scary, don't I?*) on a piece of paper and passes it to student B. Student B writes an answer (e.g. *Not really. I look much scarier!*) and passes the paper back to A.

Tag questions

We are the ghosts

(Dad, Dad, wake up!
What is it, son?
Dad, there's no such thing as ghosts, is there?
Course not.
Then why's there a lot of people dressed in sheets in our house?
What?
Look, over there …
Oh goodness me, who are you?)

We are the ghosts,
We rule the night,
We are the ghosts,
We are alright!
We are the ghosts,
We are a scream,
We are the ghosts,
The world's best team.

Ooh, ooh, ooh, ooh.
Ooh, ooh, ooh.
(Dad, who are they?)

We are the ghosts,
(Oh yeah)
We rattle chains,
We are the ghosts,
You scatterbrains.
(How rude)
We are the ghosts
(Look, Dad!)
We pass through walls
(That's clever)
We are the ghosts
Who fights us, falls.

Ooh, ooh, ooh, ooh.
Ooh, ooh, ooh.
(Are you terrified, little boy?
No, I'm not! There's no such thing as ghosts!
What? Sir Walter, show them what you can do!
Here, Dad, look! Sir Walter's taken his head off and tucked it under his arm. That's funny, isn't it, Dad? … Dad? Why have you gone all white?)

Chorus
Ooh, ooh, ooh, ooh.
Ooh, ooh, ooh.
(Here, I'm gonna sing along with you.
I'm a better singer than him,
    aren't I, Dad?)

We are the ghosts,
We play with heads,
We are the ghosts,
Live under beds.
(Look for my slippers then.)

We are the ghosts,
Night's dark and deep,
We are the ghosts,
(Best go to sleep!)

(Not yet!)

Ooh, ooh, ooh, ooh.
Ooh, ooh, ooh.

(This is fun, isn't it, Dad? Dad? –
    He's gone white as a sheet.
Maybe he's a ghost now?
Oh look, Dad, they're going. Bye!)

We are the ghosts!

(Say something, Dad.)

Tag questions

We are the ghosts | Worksheet A

1 Look at the list of things ghosts do. There are more actions listed than you hear in the song. Cross out the ones you do not hear.

dress in sheets   climb down castle walls   laugh madly
rule the night   wake everybody   fall asleep
scream   rattle chains   pass through walls
play with heads   live under beds   dress in black
break windows

2 In the song there is the sentence: *There's no such thing as ghosts, is there?* How do you say *is there* in your language?

3 Complete the following sentences with a tag question:

Ghosts pass through walls, _____?

They can take off their heads, _____?

They don't fight each other, _____?

They aren't very dangerous, _____?

A game for ghosts | Worksheet B

Tag questions

Play in pairs, or groups of three or four. Pick up a card and mime the action. The others have to guess what you're doing. If they guess correctly, you can keep the card and score one point; if they don't, put it back. If you pick up a card that matches a card you have already got, you can keep the second card and get two points.

scream	dress in sheets	play with heads	take off heads
laugh madly	rattle chains	pass through walls	live under beds
wake up everybody	break windows	climb down castle walls	fall asleep
scare people	fight people	never sleep	fly around
do not cry	do not sing	do not eat	do not play the trumpet
scream	dress in sheets	play with heads	take off heads
laugh madly	rattle chains	pass through walls	live under beds
wake up everybody	break windows	climb down castle walls	fall asleep
scare people	fight people	never sleep	fly around
do not cry	do not sing	do not eat	do not play the trumpet

Puchta/Gerngross/Holzmann/Devitt | Grammar Songs & Raps | © Helbling Languages **PHOTOCOPIABLE**

Adverbs of manner

23 Please come back

CD2 Track 11

Language focus Adverbs of manner
Level Elementary / A2
Time Lesson 1: 20 minutes
Lesson 2: (consecutive) 20 minutes
Materials CD2 – Track 11: audio recording of the song
CD2/CD-ROM part: *Please come back* Flashcards
Lesson 1: a copy of Worksheet A per student
Lesson 2: a copy of Worksheet B (questionnaire) per student

In class

Lesson 1

1. Write the following sentence on the board:

   This is Charley, the ghost. He walks _____ and he is _____ .

2. Elicit as many words from the class as would possibly fit the two gaps, e.g.

   quietly / noisily / fast / carelessly   terrible / ugly / beautiful / awful

3. Show the students the flashcards provided:

4. Elicit some language from the students, e.g. *She's friendly. He's angry*. Ask questions, e.g. *So you think he's angry. Why? What's his problem?* etc.

5. Write the following sentences on the board:

   She's a very _____ girl, and she talks _____ .
   He's often _____ . Then he talks very _____ .

   Ask your students to copy them. In a box below write *quiet / quietly / angry / angrily* and ask your students to complete the sentences.

6. You may want to quickly elicit what the difference between an adjective and an adverb is, e.g. an adjective says what someone is like; an adverb says how someone does things.

7. Hand out a copy of Worksheet A. Ask students to go through the lyrics and decide which adverb fits best in each context. When they have finished, get them to compare their results with a partner's.

8. Play the song. Students check their choices. Finally, play the song again and get the students to sing along.

Answers 1 Quietly, quietly
Angrily, angrily
happily
Lazily, lazily
Carefully, carefully
Sadly, unhappily, happily

2
X   The singer had a girlfriend. She was always very quiet.
Ch In the past he was very happy. Now he's unhappy.
2   The singer lost his friend too.
5   The singer felt lonely.
X   The singer's friend was a very angry person.
1   The singer had a girlfriend. One day she left him.
X   The singer's cat was always hungry.
4   The singer lost all his luck.
3   The singer's cat left him too.

Lesson 2

1. Hand out a copy of the questionnaire. Make sure your students understand the meaning of the adverbs.

2. Give them two or three minutes to complete the sentences about themselves. Stress that it is important that they do not just fill each sentence with an adverb, but think which adverbs express best how they do things.

3. Ask students to work in pairs. Partner A reads out the first sentence, but leaves out the adverb. Partner B has to guess the adverb. If B guesses the adverb correctly, they can write down a point. If they can't guess it, A tells them.

4. When A has read out all the sentences, they swap roles.

5. Finally, students add up their points. The student with the most points in each pair is the winner.

Extension

1   Ask students to call out adverbs of manner and write them on the board, e.g. *angrily, quietly, excitedly, noisily* etc.

2   Ask students to brainstorm verbs and verb phrases, e.g. *eat, dance, sing, walk, play the piano, paint a picture, repair my bike* etc. Write those on the board too.

3   Tell students to work in groups of four. One picks a verb and an adverb and mimes the action e.g. *repair a bike angrily*. The others have to guess what he/she is trying to show, e.g.

A: Are you opening a box?
B: No, I'm not.
C: Are you repairing your bike?
B: Yes, I am.
C: Are you doing it angrily?
B: Yes, I am.

Adverbs of manner

Please come back

Quietly, so quietly
My love one day walked up to me
And said, 'I think I'll let you be.
From now on you are free.'

Angrily, so angrily
My friend one day walked up to me
And said, 'I think I'll let you be.
From now on you are free.'

Oh no! Oh no!
Once I was living happily.
Oh no! Oh no!
My dreams are gone. How can that be?
Oh no! Oh no!
Once I was living happily.
Oh no! Oh no!
My dreams are gone. How can that be?
Oh no! Oh no!

Lazily, so lazily
My cat one day walked up to me
And said, 'I think I'll let you be.
From now on you are free.'

Carefully, so carefully
My luck one day walked up to me
And said, 'I think I'll let you be.
From now on you are free.'

Chorus

Sadly and unhappily
I'm sitting here with none but me.
Who says I wanted to be free?
Please take me, I'll come happily.

Chorus (x 2)

Please come back | Worksheet A

Adverbs of manner

1 **Circle the correct adverbs. Listen and check.**

1
Noisily / Quietly, so **noisily / quietly**
My love one day walked up to me
And said, I think I'll let you be
From now on you are free.

2
Hungrily / Angrily, so **hungrily / angrily**
My friend one day walked up to me
And said, I think I'll let you be
From now on you are free.

Chorus:
Oh no! Oh no!
Once I was living **happily / tiredly**.
Oh no! Oh no!
My dreams are gone. How can that be?
Oh no! Oh no!

3
Lazily / Carefully, so **lazily / carefully**
My cat one day walked up to me
And said, I think I'll let you be
From now on you are free.

4
Happily / Carefully, so **happily / carefully**
My luck one day walked up to me
And said, I think I'll let you be
From now on you are free.

5
Hungrily / Sadly and **unhappily / happily**
I'm sitting here with none but me.
Who says I wanted to be free?
Please take me, I'll come **lazily / happily**.

2 **Match the summaries with the verses of the song and the chorus. Fill in numbers 1–5 or CH (chorus). Careful – there are three sentences that do not match.**

- [ ] The singer had a girlfriend. She was always very quiet.
- [ ] In the past he was very happy. Now he's unhappy.
- [ ] The singer lost his friend too.
- [ ] The singer felt lonely.
- [ ] The singer's friend was a very angry person.
- [ ] The singer had a girlfriend. One day she left him.
- [ ] The singer's cat was always hungry.
- [ ] The singer lost all his luck.
- [ ] The singer's cat left him too.

Adverbs of manner

The Adverbs of Manner Questionnaire

Use adverbs to make true sentences about yourself. Then read out the sentences to a partner without the adverbs. Your partner has to guess the adverbs. Count the points.

perfectly	nervously – calmly
fantastically	terribly
angrily	loudly – quietly
beautifully	carefully – carelessly
safely – dangerously	unhappily – happily
well – badly	quickly – slowly
easily	successfully – unsuccessfully

I play ball games _____.
I eat my breakfast _____.
I eat my dinner _____.
I talk on the phone _____.
I sing _____.
I draw _____.
I do my homework _____.
I ride my bike _____.
I tidy up my room _____.
I dance _____.

feel + *adjective*

24 I'm feeling sick

CD2 Track 12

Language focus *feel* + adjective: *feel sick*; *feel ill*; *feel bad*; present perfect
Level Elementary / A2
Time 20–30 minutes
Materials CD2 – Track 12: audio recording of the song
Prepare a copy of Worksheet A, one per student (or per pair of students). Cut the worksheet in half along the dotted line. Also, copy Worksheet B, one copy per student.

In class

1. Hand out Worksheet A, 1, one per student or pair of students. Give them three minutes to think up or find any rhyming words for the words on the worksheet. Tell them to write their words on the worksheet.

2. Write one word from the worksheet on the board, e.g. *tea*. Ask students to call out the rhyming words they have written down. Write all their correct suggestions on the board.

3. Hand out Worksheet A, 2. Give students about a minute to find the rhyming pairs for the words in 1.

4. Tell them that nine of the rhyming pairs will be part of the lyrics of a song titled *I'm feeling sick*. Ask them to circle the nine rhyming pairs that they think they will hear.

5. Play the song.

6. Compare the students' findings in class.

7. Hand out a copy of Worksheet B. Tell students to complete them with rhyming words. Then play the song again and get them to check. Finally, play the song again and get students to sing along.

Answers **Worksheet A, 2**
letter = better   bed = head   flu = shoe   sick = quick
mail = pale   nurse = worse   ill = pill   goat = coat
tried = cried   pain = rain   frog = dog
tea = see   hot = pot   phone = alone
bad = sad   toes = nose   snake = cake

Answers **Worksheet B**
See lyrics

Note Howard Gardner stresses that an interest in rhyme is an important part of the linguistic intelligence.

feel + adjective

I'm feeling sick

As I've written in my letter
I'm not getting better.
As I've told you in my mail
I'm looking rather pale.

I feel so ill, so ill, so ill,
Give me a pink, a pink pill.
I feel so sick, so sick, so sick,
I need one, please be quick, quick, quick.

(Oh dear!)

I'm feeling really bad,
Oh, I am very sad.
I've got a headache too –
I think I've got the flu.

Chorus

I've texted you, I've cried,
There are lots of things I've tried.
I've said it on the phone,
I'm tired and alone.

Chorus (x 2)

I feel so ill, so ill, so ill,
I don't want any pill.
Just come and visit me
And I'll feel good, you'll see.
(repeat x 2)

I feel so ill, so ill, so ill,
So ill, so ill.

COME AND VISIT ME!

feel + adjective

I'm feeling sick | Worksheet A

1 Write words that rhyme with the words below.

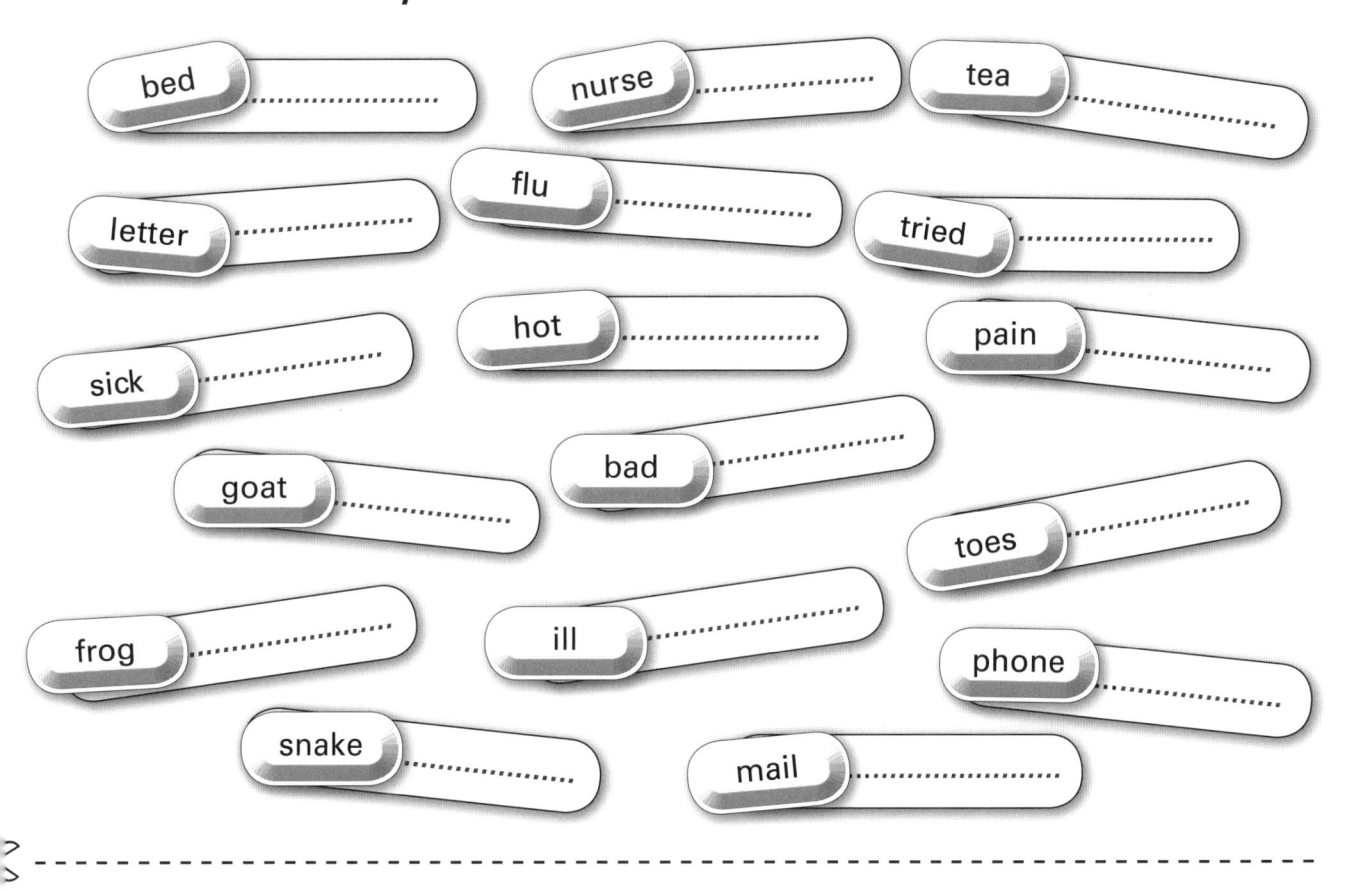

- bed ....
- nurse ....
- tea ....
- letter ....
- flu ....
- tried ....
- hot ....
- pain ....
- sick ....
- goat ....
- bad ....
- toes ....
- frog ....
- ill ....
- phone ....
- snake ....
- mail ....

---

2 Write the rhymes from 1 above.

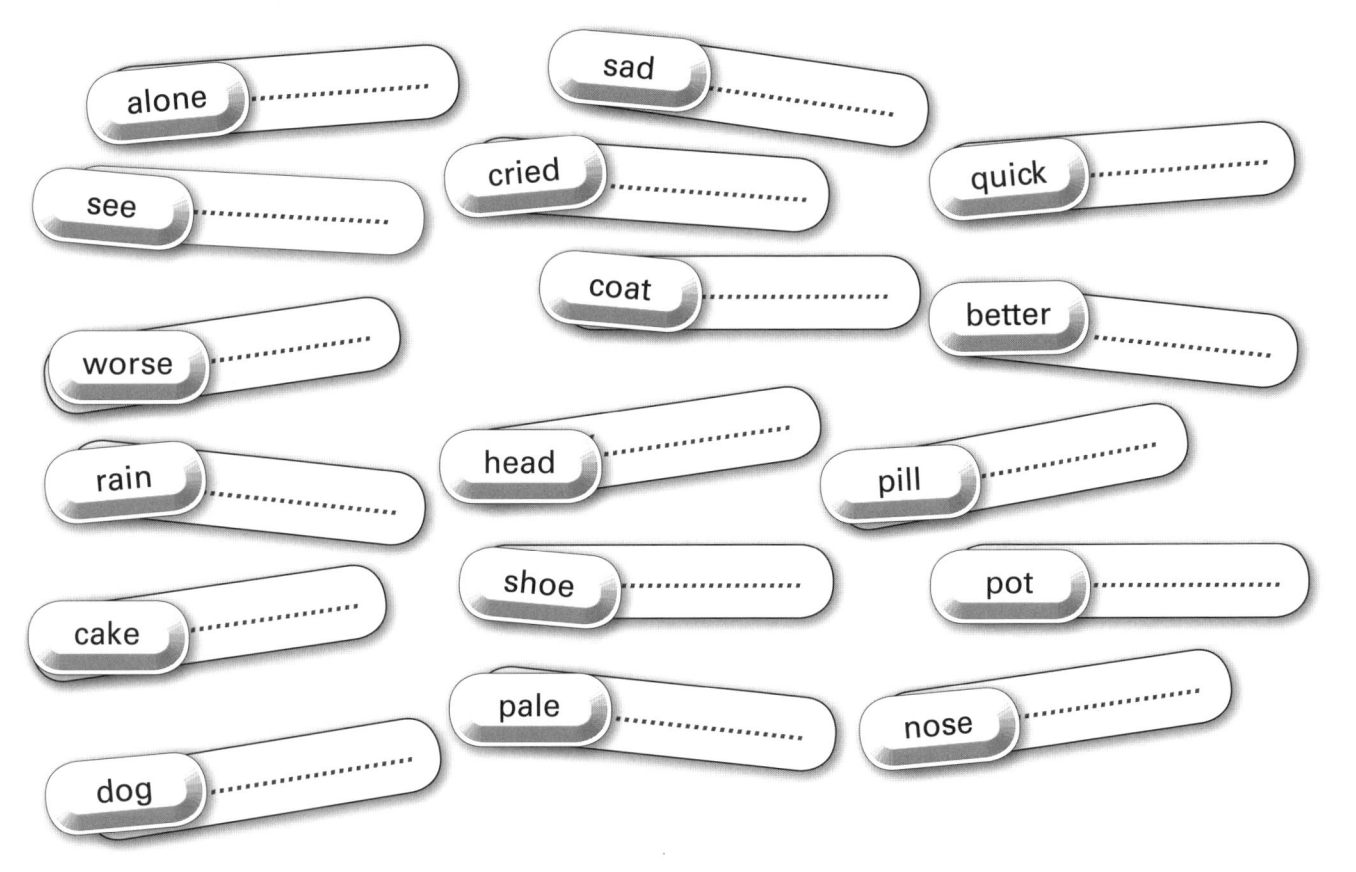

- alone ....
- sad ....
- see ....
- cried ....
- quick ....
- coat ....
- better ....
- worse ....
- rain ....
- head ....
- pill ....
- cake ....
- shoe ....
- pot ....
- pale ....
- nose ....
- dog ....

Puchta/Gerngross/Holzmann/Devitt | Grammar Songs & Raps | © Helbling Languages **PHOTOCOPIABLE**

feel + adjective

I'm feeling sick | Worksheet B

Complete with rhyming words.

I'm feeling sick
As I've written in my _____
I'm not getting _____.
As I've told you in my _____
I'm looking rather _____.

I'm feeling really _____,
Oh, I am very _____.
I've got a headache _____ –
I think I've got the _____.

I've texted you, I've _____,
There are lots of things I've _____.
I've said it on the _____,
I'm tired and _____.

I feel so ill, so ill, so _____,
I don't want any _____.
Just come and visit _____.
And I'll feel good, you'll _____.

I feel so ill, so ill, so _____,
Give me a pink, a pink _____.
I feel so sick, so sick, so _____,
I need one, please be _____.

about video games

25 It's only a game

CD2 Track 13

Language focus	Talking about video games
Level	Elementary / A2
Time	Lesson 1: 20 minutes
	Lesson 2: 20–30 minutes
Materials	CD2 – Track 13: audio recording of the song
	Lesson 1: a copy of Worksheet A per student; if possible, bring in a PC or video game, or a picture of one.
	Lesson 2: a copy of the lyrics for each student; a copy of Worksheet B per student

In class

Lesson 1

1. Hold up your PC/video game or picture, or write *PC and video games* on the board. Ask the students what they can say about these games.

2. Ask them whether they play any PC or video games. Ask them what they like about them. Elicit short answers only. (*It's great. It's thrilling.* etc.)

3. Hand out Worksheet A and tell the students that the stanzas are in the wrong order and that there is one stanza too many. Tell them to number the stanzas in the correct order and cross out the one they don't hear. Then play the song.

4. Check in class that everybody has the stanzas in the correct order and the extra one has been crossed out.

5. Then tell them you will play the song again and ask them to replace the two wrong words in each stanza with the correct words. Play the song; it may be necessary to pause the CD occasionally, so they can write down the words.

6. Ask the students to check their solutions in pairs. If there is any disagreement, ask for the correct solution in class.

Answers Correct order of verse: 2, X, 4, 3, 1
1 The stanza to be crossed out is: Treasures, maidens fair …
2 are, good, -, -, off, tell, magic, guys, helmet, on

Lesson 2

1. Hand out the lyrics and play the song again. Ask the students to sing along (with an extra group for the chorus).

about video games

2. Hand out Worksheet B. Tell the students to take the worksheet and a pencil, and walk around in class asking each other the questions, e.g.:

   A: *Can you name a PC game?*
   B: *Yes.*
   A: *Which one?*
   B: *Monkey Island.*

   Ask them to try and find at least two other students who answer *Yes*, and ask them to make notes on their worksheets.

3. While students are asking each other questions, walk around and make sure they're using English in their activity. Help them with asking questions should there be any problems. This should take up to 10–15 minutes.

4. Ask a few students about their results. Find out in which cases it was easy or difficult to find somebody.

Note This type of activity can be adapted for all kinds of topics. You can also leave 2–3 blanks in this game, where students have to put in questions of their own.

It's only a game

Helmet on your head,
Joystick in your hand,
Switch it on, and hey,
Off to Wizardland!

There you are the King.
Wizards good and bad
Follow your command
In a world so mad.

*I have already played this game, my friends,
And I can tell you how it ends.
I have already played this game, my friends,
And I can tell you how it ends.*

Helmet on your head,
Joystick in your hand,
Switch it on, and hey,
Off to Wizardland!

Magic all around,
Dangers on the road.
Evil guys and ghosts,
Flashlight: OVERLOAD!

Chorus

Time to go back home,
You switch off the screen.
And you tell your friends
About the things you've seen.

Chorus (x 2)

It's only a game | Worksheet A

1 Listen to the song and put the stanzas in the correct order. There is one stanza too many. Cross it out.

2 Then listen again. In each stanza there are two wrong words. Correct them.

☐ There you *were* _____ the King.
Wizards *old* _____ and bad
Follow your command
In a world so mad.

☐ Treasures, *maidens* _____ fair,
Dragons, *horses* _____ , swords
Wish I was still there
With the fighting hordes.

☐ Time to go back home,
You switch *on* _____ the screen.
And you *told* _____ your friends
About the things you've seen.

☐ *Evil* _____ all around,
Dangers on the road.
Evil *girls* _____ and ghosts,
Flashlight: OVERLOAD!

☐ *Cap* _____ on your head,
Joystick in your hand,
Switch it *off* _____ , and hey,
Off to Wizardland!

about video games

It's only a game | Worksheet B

Walk around and try to find at least two names of classmates for each question. Ask, for example: *Do you play PC and video games?* If the answer is *Yes*, ask a second question using the question word in brackets. For example: *Which game do you play?*

Take notes on your worksheet.

Questions	Name(s)
Find someone who:	
plays PC and video games. *(Which?)*	
can name two well-known games. *(Which?)*	
spends more than 3 hours a day playing video games. *(How long?)*	
hates PC and video games. *(Why?)*	
has never heard of the game "Battlefield." *(Heard of any other?)*	
reads fantasy books. *(Which?)*	
can name a wizard from a book or film. *(Who?)*	
can name a famous sword? *(Which?)*	
has got a helmet. *(What for?)*	
believes in ghosts. *(What kind of ghosts?)*	
isn't allowed to play PC and video games. *(Would they like to?)*	
would like to be a king/a queen *(Of what?)*	

So / Neither am / ...

26 Whatever you can do
a rap

CD2 Track 14/15

Language focus So / Neither am / do / have I

Level Elementary / A2

Time Lesson 1: 20 minutes
Lesson 2: 20 minutes

Materials CD2 - Track 14: audio recording of the rap
CD2 - Track 15: karaoke version of the rap
Lesson 1: a copy of the lyrics for each student; a copy of Worksheet A per student
Lesson 2: a copy of the lyrics for each student; prepare a copy of Worksheet B, and have a pair of scissors, per group of four. Prepare small pieces of paper with either a plus or a minus sign on each, one piece per student; so if you have 24 students, that's 6 worksheets and scissors, and 12 plus signs and 12 minus signs.

In class

Lesson 1

1. Write a sentence on the board, e.g.: *I'm very good at playing chess*. Ask students whether they are good at it, too. Elicit answers in both the negative and the positive.

   They will probably reply with *Yes, I am. / No, I'm not.*

2. Revise the structure *So am I / So have I / So do I*. Write examples on the board, e.g.:
   I'm good at badminton. – So am I.
   I like yoghurt for breakfast. – So do I.
   I have many CDs. – So have I.

   Say sentences, e.g. *I like detective stories,* and ask those students who also like them to answer with *So do I*. Then continue, using the structures *I'm ...* and *I have ....*

   Repeat the procedure with negative sentences. Revise the structure *Neither am I / Neither have I / Neither do I.*

3. Practise the structures with a few mini-dialogues in the form of a short drill. A student says a sentence, e.g. *I'm 12 years old*, and points at another student, who replies with the appropriate structure, e.g. *So am I.*

4. Hand out Worksheet A and play the rap, more than once if necessary, and ask the students to tick the things they hear. Stop the CD whenever necessary so students have time to do the task. Then ask them to write the correct phrases against each sentence. (The answers do not have to be true for them. They are just practising the structure.)

5. Check the answers in class. Let students read out each mini-dialogue in pairs.

So / Neither am / ...

Answers

Ticked sentences:
I'm good at tennis. So am I.
I'm good at football. So am I.
I'm a star on TV. So am I.

Unticked:
I've got a red mountain bike. So have I.
I'm a computer expert. So am I.
I love PC games. So do I.
I run a mile in four minutes. So do I.

I don't need to learn for school. Neither do I.
I always remember what I hear. So do I.
I don't have to study. Neither do I.

I haven't got a computer. Neither have I.
I haven't got any problems at school. Neither have I.
I don't play silly PC games. Neither do I.
I don't read a lot. Neither do I.
I haven't got any PC games. Neither have I.

Lesson 2

1. Hand out the lyrics and play the rap, asking the students to join in (one group takes part A, another group takes part B).

2. Hand out Worksheet B. Students get together in groups of four.

3. The students cut up their 24 cards and distribute 6 to every member. Assign each student a plus or a minus by giving each one a little piece of paper with either a plus or a minus sign on it, so that in each group you have two plus and two minus students. Then the students walk around and say their sentences to each other. When Student A says a sentence, B has to answer correctly, as follows:

    With affirmative sentences, if B has got a plus sign, they answer with *So am / do / have I*. If B has a minus sign, they say: *I'm not / I don't / I haven't* etc.

    With negative sentences, if B has a minus sign, they answer: *Neither am / do / have I*. If B has a plus sign, they answer: *I do / I have / I am*.

    For example: If A says to B, a plus-student: *I'm good at tennis,* B replies *So am I*. If A says that sentence to B, a minus-student, B replies: *I'm not*. If A gets a correct reply then they score a point. If A gets any other answer, they take off a point. Note that it is always A, the person who asks, who gets/takes off points.

4. Play the game for about five minutes. Tell the students to keep score on one of their pieces of paper or by memorizing it. Then see who has got the highest score.

Note If you collect all the cards when the game is over, you can use them for revision another time.

Extension

Use the karaoke version as suggested on pp. 7-8.

Whatever you can do

A: *Whatever you can do,*
I can do it much better than you.
B: *Whatever you say, hey,*
I say I am better than you!

A: I've got the latest racing car.
B: So have I. But I've got three.
A: I'm good at tennis and football too.
B: So am I. I'm a star on TV.

Chorus

(Break it down)

Monday, Tuesday, Wednesday, Thursday, Friday, Saturday, Sunday too –
These are the days of the week, my friend, when I am better than you.

A: I don't need to learn for school.
B: Neither do I. I am so cool and clever,
I always remember what I hear.
Do I have to study? No, never.

A: Whatever you can do,
I can do it much better than you.
B: Whatever you say, I'm better
Because I am better than you.

A: I am better than you!
B: I am better than you!
(repeat x 3)

So / Neither am / ...

Whatever you can do | Worksheet A

1 Listen to the rap and tick the things you can hear.

✓	I've got the latest racing car.	So have I.
☐	I've got a red mountain bike.	_____
☐	I haven't got a computer.	_____
☐	I haven't got any problems at school.	_____
☐	I'm a computer expert.	_____
☐	I love PC games.	_____
☐	I don't play silly PC games.	_____
☐	I'm a star on TV.	_____
☐	I don't need to learn for school.	_____
☐	I run a mile in four minutes.	_____
☐	I always remember what I hear.	_____
☐	I don't read a lot.	_____
☐	I don't have to study.	_____
☐	I'm good at tennis.	_____
☐	I'm good at football.	_____
☐	I haven't got any PC games.	_____

2 Then listen again and write *So do / am / have I* or *Neither do / am / have I* against each sentence.

So / Neither am / ...

So and neither cards | Worksheet B

First get together in groups of four. Cut up the cards.

Each of you takes 6 cards, walks around and says a sentence from your cards to another student. If you get a reply with the correct use of *So am / have / do I* or *Neither am / do / have I*, you get one point; if you get any other reply you have to take off one point.

Play for five minutes. Keep track of your score on a piece of paper or by adding it up in your head.

I'm a TV star.	I like spaghetti for breakfast.
I don't drink fizzy drinks.	I don't watch the news.
I don't need to study for school.	I don't go to parties during the week.
I'm good at tennis.	I'm brilliant at Maths.
I'm a great swimmer.	I'm not good at drawing.
I ride my bike to school every day.	I don't play in an orchestra.
I don't sing in the shower.	I listen to my MP3 player when doing my homework.
I like reading.	I don't like getting up early.
I'm a good chess player.	I'm a pretty good footballer.
I don't know where Zimbabwe is.	I've got a lot of DVDs.
I haven't got any money.	I've got a friend in Turkey.
I didn't do my English homework.	I always do the dishes.

Puchta/Gerngross/Holzmann/Devitt | Grammar Songs & Raps | © Helbling Languages **PHOTOCOPIABLE**

ever and never

27 Have you ever...?

CD2 Track 16

Language focus	Present perfect with *ever* and *never*
Level	Elementary / A2 upwards
Time	Lesson 1: 20 minutes
	Lesson 2: about 30 minutes
Materials	CD2 – Track 16: audio recording of the song
	Lesson 1: a copy of Worksheet A per student
	Lesson 2: a copy of the lyrics for each student; a copy of Worksheet B per student

In class

Lesson 1

1. Write the following skeleton sentences on the board and ask the students to guess what they mean:

   A: H_____ y_____ e_____ b_____ t____ L_____?
   B: N__, I h_____, b____ I'_____ b_____ t___ M_____ .

   Ask the students to call out words starting with the letters they can see. Whenever they call out a word that is part of the sentences, write it on the board. It's important that you keep a non-judgemental attitude when the students call out 'incorrect' words. In fact, make sure students understand that there are no 'incorrect' words, only words that don't fit the gaps.

   Don't rush this, as students may need time to think.

2. When students have guessed the correct sentences (*A: Have you ever been to London? B: No, I haven't, but I've been to Manchester.*), hand out a copy of Worksheet A to each student. Get them to match the sentence halves. Allow two or three minutes for this.

3. When students have finished, play the song to them. Get them to compare their results with the lyrics.

Answer See lyrics.

Lesson 2

1. Hand out a copy of Worksheet B. Show the students how to make sentences starting with *Have you ever...?* using the prompts on the worksheet.

2. Tell them to work in pairs and find as many sentences starting with *Have you ever...?* as possible. Tell them that if they can make a meaningful sentence from the prompts, they'll get one point. They'll get three points for any meaningful sentence they can make starting with *Have you ever...?* without using the prompts. Tell them that you'll give them three minutes to do this.

3. Stop them after three minutes. Get students to read out their sentences. Say *point* whenever a pair have created a meaningful sentence using the prompts on the worksheet, or *three points* for any meaningful sentence they have created without using the prompts.

4. Ask students to work in groups. One student begins, asking a *Have you ever...?* question. The student on their right answers the question. If the answer is *yes*, they could elaborate a bit, depending on the level of language. If the answer is *no*, a short, simple answer – *No, I haven't* – is OK.

5. The student who has given the answer is the next one to ask a question. For example:

   S1: *Have you ever found some money?*
   S2: *No, I haven't.*
   S2: *Have you ever broken an arm or a leg?*
   S3: *Yes. When I was three, I broke my right arm.*
   S3: *Have you ever...?*

Have you ever...?

Have you ever been a hero
Where you flew down from the sky?
Have you ever danced calypso?
Have you given it a try?

I've never even dreamt of it.
I wouldn't like it, not a bit!
Have you never ever even tried?

Have you ever been a heroine?
Have you sailed the ocean far and wide?
Have you travelled in a time machine?
Have you ever, ever tried?

Chorus

Have you never had the wildest dreams?
Have you never tried to get to the moon?
You have never ever so it seems.
Then it's time to start, and please start soon.
And please start soon.

I've never been on mountains.
I've never been to sea.
I've never swum in fountains.
I've never climbed a tree.

What have you ever done?
Just tell me one oh one.
Tell me one good thing you've
    ever done.

I've never run in races.
I've never scored a goal.
I've never seen foreign places.
And never danced rock 'n' roll.

What have you ever done?
Just tell me one oh one –
Tell me one good thing you've
    ever done.
Tell me one good thing you've
    ever done.

ever and never

Have you ever...? | Worksheet A

Match the sentence halves. Write the letter in the box.

1	Have you ever been			A	it a try?
2	Where you flew			B	danced calypso?
3	Have you ever			C	a hero?
4	Have you given			D	down from the sky?

Chorus

1	I've never even			A	dreamt of it.
2	I wouldn't like it,			B	ever even tried?
3	Have you never			C	not a bit!

1	Have you ever been			A	the ocean far and wide?
2	Have you sailed			B	ever tried?
3	Have you travelled			C	a heroine?
4	Have you ever,			D	in a time machine?

1	Have you never had			A	and please start soon.
2	Have you never tried			B	so it seems.
3	You have never ever			C	to get to the moon?
4	Then it's time to start,			D	the wildest dreams?

1	I've never been			A	to sea.
2	I've never been			B	in fountains.
3	I've never swum			C	on mountains.
4	I've never climbed			D	a tree.

1	What have			A	one oh one –
2	Just tell me			B	you've ever done.
3	Tell me one good thing			C	you ever done?

1	I've never run			A	scored a goal.
2	I've never			B	in races.
3	I've never seen			C	rock 'n' roll.
4	And never danced			D	foreign places.

ever and never

Have you ever...? | Worksheet B

1. How many sentences starting with *Have you ever...?* can you make with a partner?

2. Then play the *Have you ever...?* game.

see a shooting star	sing karaoke	climb to the highest point in your country	break an arm or a leg
live in another country	be in the USA	go to a circus	lose your mobile
meet a famous person	cook a meal for your family	win a prize	ride a horse
be alone for a day	be scared of an animal	dream of flying	be in London
eat frogs legs	have an accident	find some money	be unable to stop laughing

will-future

28 The weatherman
a rap

CD2 Track 17/18

Language focus	*will*-future, weather words
Level	Elementary / A2 upwards
Time	Lesson 1: 15–20 minutes
	Lesson 2: (consecutive) 15–20 minutes
Materials	CD2 – Track 17: audio recording of the rap
	CD2 – Track 18: karaoke version of the rap
	Lesson 1: a copy of Worksheet A for each student.
	Lesson 2: a copy of Worksheet B for each student.

In class

Lesson 1

1. Tell your students that they are going to look at a nonsense rap text. Hand out a copy of Worksheet A to each student. Ask them if they can find any of the nonsense bits in the text and underline them. Allow 2–3 minutes for this.

2. Ask students to call out the bits that they believe are nonsense.

3. Tell students that you are going to play the rap with the correct lyrics. They should first only listen, and underline the bits on their worksheets that are different from what they hear.

4. Play the rap again. This time get students to jot down in the margin of the worksheet the correct language. This will take some time, and you may want to stop the audio player several times so students have time to make their notes.

5. Repeat this several times until students are confident that they've got the correct lyrics. Compare the students' version of the text with the original below.

Answer
The nonsense words are:
in May, hooray, eat a kiwi or two, old Heather
lawn mowers, flowers, play, Fred
wonder, pain, rain
towers, flowers, panda, hop
worms, Sophie's show, worms, Joe, ride
I'm really hungry Sue, I've made some pizza just for you, cows, there'll be a line, mine
French fries, everyone, sun

Lesson 2

1. Give each student a copy of Worksheet B. Make sure they understand the language. Get them to study the verb phrases and remember them.

2. Put students in groups of four. Tell each student to tick six actions that they'll probably do tonight. Tell them not to show their choices to any other student.

3. Explain the game to the class. One student in each group starts, and each other student in the group writes a list of the six actions that they think that student

will-future

will probably do tonight. When they have finished, that student tells them what she/he has marked in step 2, for example:

I'll probably look after my pet. etc.

4. Each time another student in the group has made a correct guess, they tick it off their list.

5. The game is over when each student in the group has told the others about what they'll probably do tonight. The students in the group count their ticks. The one with the most ticks is the winner.

Extension

Use the karaoke version as suggested on pp. 7-8.

The weatherman

Hey, let's have a BBQ
Outside in the garden, me and you.
But first, let's turn the TV on
And see what the weather's going to do.

What will the weatherman say?
What will the weather be like today?
What will the weatherman say?
What will the weather be like today?

There'll be some showers today
(There'll be some showers today),
So why not stay stay stay
(So why not stay)
In bed?

Chorus

There'll be some thunder and some rain
(There'll be some thunder and some rain).
Oh what a pain pain pain
As he said …

Chorus

(There'll be some rain, there'll be some showers
Yes, the rain will pour for hours and hours
There'll be some thunder and lots of rain,
Then it'll stop but start again.)
(repeat)

There'll be some storms and lots of snow
(Storms and snow will come down from the north).
Why don't we go go go
And hide?

Wait, I've got good news for you.
We've heard the skies will soon turn blue.
The clouds will go, the sun will shine.
Listen to the weatherman, it's going to be fine!

There'll be blue skies and lovely sun
(There'll be blue skies and lovely sun).
Hey, we'll have fun fun fun
(Have fun)
Outside!

That's what the weatherman will say,
That's what the weather will be like today…
That's what the weatherman will say,
That's what the weather will be like today…
That's what the weatherman will say,
That's what the weather will be like today…
That's what the weather will be like today,
That's what the weatherman will say.

will-future

The weatherman | Worksheet A

This rap includes some parts that don't make sense. Find those parts and underline them.

What will we do in May?
I'd like to go outside, hooray!
OK let's eat a kiwi or two
And see what old Heather's going to do.

Chorus:
What will the weatherman say?
What will the weather be like today?
What will the weatherman say?
What will the weather be like today?

There'll be lawn mowers today
(There'll be some flowers today)
So why not play play play
(So why not play)
With Fred?

There'll be some wonder and some pain
(There'll be some wonder and some pain)
Oh what a rain rain rain
As he said …

There'll be some rain, there'll be some towers
Yes, the rain will pour for flowers and flowers
There'll be a panda and lots of rain,
Then I'll hop but start again.

There'll be some worms in Sophie's show
(Worms and Joe will come down from the north).
Why don't we go go go
For a ride?

Wait! – I'm really hungry, Sue.
I've made some pizza just for you.
The cows will go, there'll be a line.
Listen to the weatherman, it's going to be mine!

There'll be French fries for everyone
(There'll be French fries for everyone).
Hey, there'll be sun sun sun
(Lots of sun)
Inside.

That's what the weatherman will say,
That's what the weather will be like today…

136 PHOTOCOPIABLE Puchta/Gerngross/Holzmann/Devitt | Grammar Songs & Raps | © Helbling Languages

I'll probably... | Worksheet B

Which six of these actions will you probably do tonight? Tick ✓ six actions. Don't show them to your group.

will-future

- watch TV
- read a book
- study for a test
- write emails
- talk to a friend on my mobile
- surf the web
- hang out with friends
- listen to music
- do a hobby
- sit and think
- help my mum and dad
- look after a pet

Quick-reference guide

This guide will help you select an activity suitable for your class based on the time you have available, the learning level(s) of your students, and the language focus.

To use it, look down the 'Lesson time' column till you come to a time that's suitable for you, and then look across to see the name of the activity in the range of levels it's suited to. Then across again to find language focus and the page number.

If you prefer to start with the level of your students, find the level on the top line, then go downwards till you find an activity name, and on that same row you will find the time required, the language focus and the page number.

Please note that the guidance is very basic; it allows you to see, when you're thinking of running an activity for the first time, how long it is likely to take according to the authors' experience. You're free to change the time of any activity or expand its level according to your preference.

Beginners A1	Post-beginners A1	Elementary A2	and upwards	Language focus	Lesson time (mins)	Audio CD	Flashcard CD2/CD-ROM part	Page number
	There's a monster in the forest			*There is/there are*	30 + 20	✓	✓	9
To be party				Forms of *to be*	30 + 25	✓	✓	14
	Are you happy?			Forms of *to be*; negative and questions; vocabulary: feelings	20 + 30	✓	✓	19
	Find the gnomes, Sherlock Groans			Present simple	45 + 25	✓	✓	23
	Tea rap			3rd person singular present simple	15 + 15	✓	✓	28
	Pizza rap			Negation, 3rd person singular present simple	30 + 30	✓	✓	32
The hungry monster rap				*a/an*	20 + 10	✓	✓	36
	Generous Joe song			Object pronouns	20 + 30	✓	✓	40
	Peggy Sue			Question words	30 + 30	✓	✓	44
	Midnight on Blueberry Hill			Present continuous	20 + 30	✓	✓	49
	Robbery at Hanbury Hall			Past tense of *to be* + questions	20 + 20	✓		54
	The story's on TV			Past tense	15 + 15	✓		59
	The lion song			Vocabulary: animals	20 + 15	✓	✓	64
	The *going to* song			*going to*, to express future time	20 + 30	✓	✓	68
		The Western star		Past tense for narration	20–30 + 20–30	✓	✓	72
		The Gang of Four		Past tense questions	20–30 + 20–30	✓		77
		The badbad beasts		Comparison of adjectives (superlatives)	15 + 15	✓	✓	82
		All my *have-tos*		*Have to*	20 + 20	✓		88
		I'm not going to …		*Not going to*	20 + 20	✓		93
		The *some* and *any* rap		*Some, any*	20 + 20	✓	✓	97
		The pyramids		Past tense	20 + 20	✓		102
		We are the ghosts		Tag questions	20 + 20	✓		107
		Please come back		Adverbs of manner	20 + 20	✓	✓	112
		I'm feeling sick		*Feel* + adjective; present perfect	20–30	✓		117
		It's only a game		Talking about video games	20 + 20–30	✓		121
		Whatever you can do		*So/Neither am/do /have I*	20 + 20	✓		125
			Have you ever … ?	Present perfect with *ever* and *never*	20 + 30	✓		130
			The weatherman	*Will*-future, weather words	15–20 + 15–20	✓		134

Puchta/Gerngross/Holzmann/Devitt | Grammar Songs & Raps | © Helbling Languages **PHOTOCOPIABLE**

CD contents list

CD1 CD 1 TRACK LIST

01	There's a monster in the forest *(a rap)*	01:40
02	There's a monster in the forest *(karaoke version)*	01:42
03	*To be* party *(a rap)*	02:47
04	*To be* party *(karaoke version)*	02:48
05	Are you happy? *(a rap)*	01:39
06	Are you happy? *(karaoke version)*	01:44
07	Find the gnomes, Sherlock Groans	01:53
08	Tea rap	02:02
09	Tea rap *(karaoke version)*	02:01
10	Pizza rap	01:18
11	Pizza rap *(karaoke version)*	01:20
12	The hungry monster rap	02:16
13	The hungry monster rap *(karaoke version)*	02:18
14	Generous Joe song	01:43
15	Peggy Sue	02:21
16	Midnight on Blueberry Hill	03:27
17	Robbery at Hanbury Hall	02:40
18	The story's on TV	02:05
19	The lion song	02:47
20	The *going to* song	02:20

TOTAL 42:58

CD2 CD 2/AUDIO PART TRACK LIST

01	The Western star	01:59
02	The Gang of Four	02:20
03	The badbad beasts	03:09
04	All my *have-tos* *(a rap)*	01:58
05	All my *have-tos* *(karaoke version)*	01:59
06	I'm not going to …	01:54
07	The *some* and *any* rap	02:18
08	The *some* and *any* rap *(karaoke version)*	02:20
09	The pyramids	02:35
10	We are the ghosts	02:45
11	Please come back	03:34
12	I'm feeling sick	03:00
13	It's only a game	03:19
14	Whatever you can do *(a rap)*	01:37
15	Whatever you can do *(karaoke version)*	01:38
16	Have you ever …?	02:46
17	The weatherman *(a rap)*	03:02
18	The weatherman *(karaoke version)*	03:04

TOTAL 45:25

CD 2/CD-ROM PART

130 flashcards to print out